by EDUGORILLA
Your Guide To Success

Model Test Papers

ICSE Class 10

For Term 2

PHYSICS

Author:
Mr. Shivam Tiwari

Title : Model Test Papers for class -X Physics

Author Name : Mr. Shivam Tiwari

Published By : EduGorilla Community Pvt. Ltd.

Publishers Address : 12/651, First Floor Opp. Arvindo Park, Near Jama Masjid, Indira Nagar, Lucknow, Uttar Pradesh - 226016, India

Copyright

ISBN: 9789355564320

Disclaimer

Compiled and Created by EduGorilla Book Experts

Printed by EduGorilla Community Pvt. Ltd.

SYLLABUS

PHYSICS

BIFURCATED SYLLABUS

(As per the Reduced Syllabus for ICSE – Class X Year 2022 Examination)

SEMESTER 2

(Marks: 40)

S. NO.	NAME OF THE CHAPTER
1.	CALORIMETRY
2.	ELECTROMAGNETISM
3.	CURRENT ELECTRICITY
4.	SOUND
5.	RADIOACTIVITY

SCIENCE (52)

PHYSICS SCIENCE

Paper - 1CLASS X

wavelength); properties common to all electromagnetic radiations; properties and uses of infrared and ultraviolet radiation.

1. **Sound**

   (i) Natural vibrations, Damped vibrations, Forced vibrations and Resonance - a specialcase of forced vibrations. *Meaning and simple applications of natural, damped, forced vibrations and resonance.*

   (ii) Loudness, pitch and quality of sound

   Definition of each of the characteristics andfactors affecting them.

2. **Electricity and Magnetism**

   (i) Ohm's Law; concepts of emf, potential difference, resistance; resistances in series and parallel, internal resistance.

   Concepts of pd (V), current (I), resistance
   (R) and charge (Q). Ohm's law: statement, V=IR; SI units; graph of V vs I and resistance from slope; ohmic and non-ohmic resistors, factors affecting resistance

   (Including specific resistance) and internal resistance; super conductors, electromotive force (emf); combination of resistances in series and parallel. Simple numerical problems using the above relations. (Simple network of resistors including not more than four external resistors. Internal resistance may be included).

   (ii) Electrical power and energy.

   Electrical energy; examples of heater, motor, lamp, loudspeaker, etc.Electrical power; measurement of electricalenergy, W = QV = VIt from the definition ofpd. Combining with ohm's law $W = VIt = I^2 Rt = (V^2/R)\ t$ and electrical power $P = (W/t)$
   $= VI = I^2R = V^2/R$. Units: SI and commercial; Power rating of common appliances, household consumption of electric energy; calculation of total energy consumed by electrical appliances; W = Pt (kilowatt × hour = kW h) - simple numerical problems.

   (iii) Household circuits – main circuit; switches; fuses; earthing; safety precautions; three-pin plugs; colour coding of wires.

   House wiring (ring system) (diagrammatic representation excluded), main circuit (3wires-live, neutral, earth) with fuse / MCB, main switch and its advantages, need for earthing, fuse, 3-pin plug and socket;Conventional location of live, neutral and earth points in 3 pin plugs and sockets. Safety precautions, colour coding of wires.

   (iv) Magnetic effect of a current (principles only, laws not required); electromagnetic induction (elementary).

   Oersted's experiment on the magnetic effectof electric current; magnetic field (B) and field lines due to current in a straight wire (qualitative only), right hand thumb rule – magnetic field due to a current in a loop; Electromagnets: their uses; comparisons with a permanent magnet; conductor carrying current in a magnetic field experiences a force, Fleming's Left Hand Rule and its understanding, Simple introduction to electromagnetic induction; a magnet moved along the axis of a solenoid induces current, Fleming's Right Hand Ruleand its application in understanding the direction of current in a coil and Lenz's law,Comparison of AC and DC.

3. **Heat**

(i) Calorimetry: meaning, specific heat capacity; principle of method of mixtures; Numerical Problems on specific heat capacity using heat loss and gain and the method of mixtures.

Heat and its units (calorie, joule), temperature and its units (°C, K); thermal (heat) capacity $C' = Q/\Delta T$... (SI unit of C'):Specific heat Capacity $C = Q/m\Delta T$ (SI unit of C) Mutual relation between Heat Capacity and Specific Heat capacity, valuesof C for some common substances (ice, water and copper). Principle of method of mixtures including mathematical statement. Natural phenomenon involving specific heat. Consequences of high specific heat of water. [Simple numerical problems].

(ii) Latent heat; loss and gain of heat involving change of state for fusion only.

Change of phase (state); heating curve for water; latent heat; specific latent heat of fusion (SI unit). Simple numerical problems. Common physical phenomena involving latent heat of fusion.

4. **Modern Physics**

i) Radioactivity and changes in the nucleus; background radiation and safety precautions.

Brief introduction (qualitative only) of the nucleus, nuclear structure, atomic number (Z), mass number (A). Radioactivity as spontaneous disintegration. α β and γ - their nature and properties; changes within the nucleus. One example each of α and β decay with equations showing changes in Z and A. Uses of radioactivity - radio isotopes. Harmful effects. Safety precautions. Background radiation.

Radiation: X-rays; radioactive fallout from nuclear plants and other sources.

Nuclear Energy: working on safe disposal of waste. Safety measures to be strictly reinforced.

A NOTE ON SI UNITS

SI units (*System International d'Unites*) were adopted internationally in 1968.

i) Fundamental units

The system has seven fundamental (or basic) units,one for each of the fundamental quantities.

ii) Derived units

These are obtained from the fundamental units by multiplication or division; no numerical factors are involved. Some derived units with complex names are:

When the unit is named after a person, the *symbol* has a capital letter

Fundamental quantity	Unit	
	Name	**Symbol**
Mass	kilogram	kg
Length	meter	m
Time	second	s
Electric current	ampere	A
Temperature	kelvin	K
Luminous intensity	candela	cd
Amount of substance	mole	mol

iii) Standard prefixes

Decimal multiples and submultiples are attached to units when appropriate, as bel

Multiple	**Prefix**	**Symbol**
10^{9}	giga	G
10^{6}	mega	M
10^{3}	kilo	k
10^{-1}	deci	d
10^{-2}	centi	c
10^{-3}	milli	m
10^{-6}	micro	μ
10^{-9}	nano	n
10^{-12}	Pico	p
10^{-15}	femto	f

REVISION TECHNIQUE

- **WHY SHOULD YOU REVISE?**

You cannot expect to remember all the Physics that you have studied unless you revise. It is important to review all your course, so that you can answer the examination questions.

- **WHERE SHOULD YOU REVISE?**

In a quiet room, with a table and a clock. The room should be brightly lighted. A reading lamp on the table helps you to concentrate on your work and reduces eye-strain.

- **WHEN SHOULD YOU REVISE?**

Start your revision early each evening, before your brain gets tired.

- **HOW SHOULD YOU REVISE?**

If you sit down to revise without thinking of a definite finishing time, you will find that your learning efficiency falls lower and lower and lower.

If you sit down to revise, saying to yourself that you will definitely stop work after 3 hours, then your learning efficiency falls at the beginning but rises towards the end as your brain realises it is coming to the end of the session (see Graph.

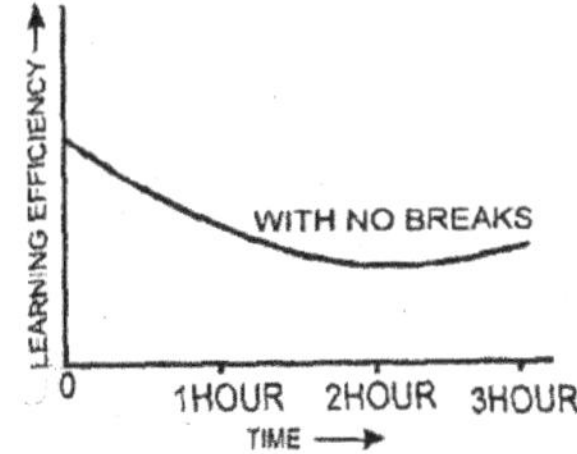

We can use this U-shaped curve to help us work more efficiently by splitting a 3-hour session into 3 shorter sessions, each of about 50 minutes with short, planned breaks between them.

The breaks must be planned beforehand so that the graph rises near the end of each short session [Graph

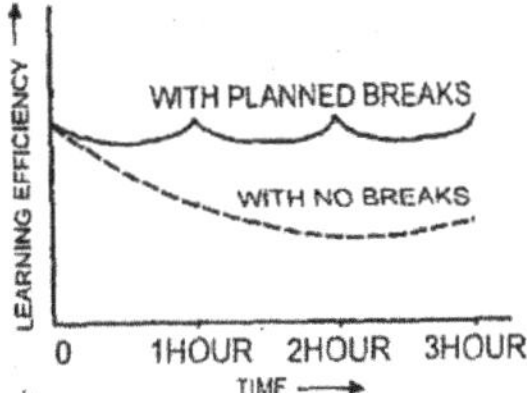

II] *how much you gain:*

For example, if you start your revision at 6.00 p.m. you should look at your clock or watch and say to yourself, 1 will work until 7.00 p.m. and then stop — neither earlier and nor later'

At 7.00 p.m. you should leave the table for a relaxation break of 10 minutes (or less), returning by 7.10 p.m. when you should say to yourself, 1 will work until 8.10 p.m. and then stop neither earlier and nor later.'

Continuing in this way is more efficient and causes less strain on you. You get through more work and you feel less tired.

- **HOW OFTEN SHOULD YOU REVISE?**

The adjoining graphs show the amount of information that your memory can recall at different times after you have finished a revision session

the graph rises at the beginning. This is because, your brain is still sorting out the information that you have been learning

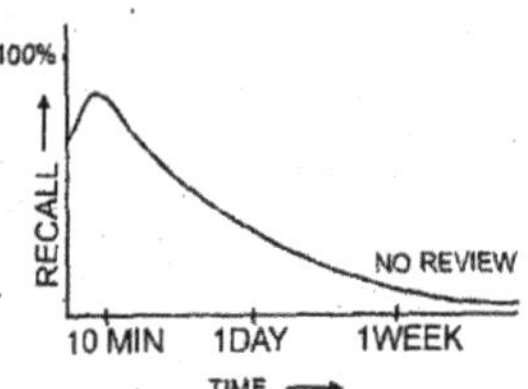

The graph soon falls rapidly so that after 1 day you may remember only about a quarter of what you had learned [Graph 1111.

There are two ways of

improving your recall process and raising this graph

1. If you briefly revise the same work again after 10 minutes (at the high point of the graph) then the graph falls much more slowly [Graph IV).

This fits in with your 10-minute break between revision sessions.

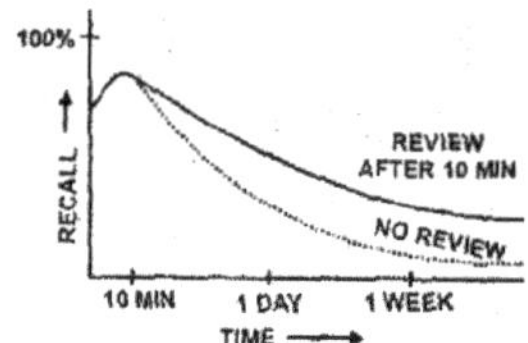

Using the example on the last page, when you return to your table at 7.10 p.m. the first thing you should do is revie briefly, the work you learned before 7.00 pm

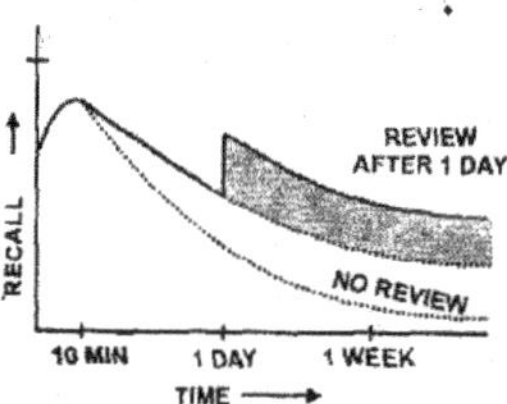

The graph can be lifted again by briefly reviewing the work after I day and then again after I week. That is, on Tuesday night you should look through the work you learned on Monday night and the work you learned on the previous Tuesday night, so that it is fixed quite firmly in your long-term memory [Graphs V and Vl].

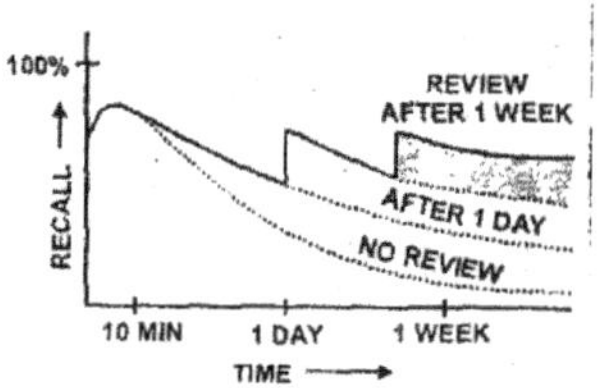

2. Another method of improving your memory is by taking care to try to understand all parts of your work. This makes all the graphs rise higher.

   If you learn your work in a parrot-fashion (as you have to do with telephone numbers), all these graphs will be lower. On the occasions when you have to learn facts by heart, try to picture them as exaggerated, colorful images in 'our mind

REMEMBER

The most important points about revision are that it must occur often and be repeated at the right intervals.

- **TIPS FOR YOUR BOARD EXAMINATION.**

The moment Board Examinations stealthily approach the lives of students, many of them start panicking about the huge syllabus, preparation, revision and the result thereof Students start getting nervous just before the exams, and start searching for ways to release their paranoia. To release then with such stress and tension please follow some steps given below for 10" Board Examination Preparation.

I - The first step for every student should be to get a thorough knowledge of the latest syllabus by referring to the ICSE COUNCIL. After that, they should make a time table for themselves which would provide them with a sehedule that would help them plan their syllabus and concentrate better.

2 -The one thing that students should note before sitting down to study is to make sure that the place in which they are going to study is free from gadgets like computer, TV, radio , mobile etc. Another thing that equally needs to be avoided is talking with friends while studying; they can do so when they are finished with studying or when they are free.

3. Students are also provided with previous year sample papers by many publications which can be of great help as they can be solved on an everyday basis. They help in analyzing the mistakes that are being committed and that can be worked upon. By having the latest papers students get an idea of the type of questions expected, and the level of difficulty in the Board Exam.

4. In order to score high marks students tend to revert to the use of malpractices. In many cases, they cram down the syllabus, instead of trying to understand it. They need to undersf and that both of these methods are wrong in the present and for the future. Cramming without understanding, will take them nowhere and using wrong means can lead to them being caught and not being able to attempt the paper.

5. In order to feel fresh and energetic the whole day, students should always eat and sleep well. They should always have an early dinner and should not study till late night (specially a night before the exam). Fast food and greasy food should be avoided as much as possible and a habit of getting up early to study should be adopted.

6. Making notes and practicing all the problems by writing them down rather than verbally learn in them is one of the best tricks to remember and understand the course. Students can also make brief notes of every chapter so that they can refer to them without needing to open their textbook every time.

7. Taking help when in doubt or in any kind of problem should be done by the students well on time. Doubts can be cleared by meeting the concerned teachers, friends and seniors.

8. The idea of not taking breaks in between and studying continually is a mistake often committed by students.

9. Students should avoid mood swings and personal problems that may prevent them from studying and completing their work. They should always try and remain in a jolly and happy mood and ignore the problems that come in their way. This will help them concentrate better.

10. Students should always learn and practice time management. They should work on their writing speed so that they can write fast and neat and not miss any questions while attempting the paper.

11. Don't neglect your health. Just because you're short of time doesn't mean you should live on junk foodie Try to get your fruits and vegetables every day. Remember to exercise at least 30 minutes a day. Doing these things will support mental, physical and emotional function:

12. It's not a good idea to pick up your books and start working until you're finished— because you may not have enough time to accomplish all your tasks. Figure out how much time you have for each assignment, and plot this out in your calendar. Try to give yourself some extra time for each assignment in case one takes longer than you expected. When you plot out your time, be sure to schedule in study breaks. Working straight through without a break can make you less efficient and somewhat insane.

13. Set a time limit on how long you study for each class. Don't go overboard on one subject and forget that you have several others to catch up on before going to bed. Also, don't rush through studying; take your time and concentrate. You may want to set an alarm clock at a certain hour, so when it rings, go to another subject, and reset the alarm.

14. Get at least 6 hours of sleep. If you have more or less sleep than you should have, you may start lacking in your coursework and become lazy because of the urge or want to sleep.

INDEX

ICSE X physics

SOLVED QUESTION PAPERS

UNSOLVED QUESTION PAPERS

1 CALORIMETRY

It is the branch of Physics in which we deal with the of quantity of heat.

Calorimeter: - The device which in used for measuring heat.

Heat [Thermal] Energy: - The sum of kinetic energy of all molecule contained in a body is called thermal energy.

"Body Possess heat energy in the form of internal kinetic unit SI unit Joule(J)"

Common unit: calorie (Cal).

* Kilo Calorie (K Cal) = 1000 Cal

1 Calorie: - Heat energy required to raise the temperature 1 g of water from 14.5^0 C - 15.5^0 C {water shows uniform After 14.5^0C}

* Food energy is also measured in calorie.
  1 Cal = 4.18 J or 4.2 J

Temperature: - Average of internal kinetic energy of molecules in an object.

Unit SI ⟶ Kelvin (K)

Common unit ⟶ Degree centigrade (^{0}C)

Clerical unit ⟶ Fahrenheit (^{0}F)

Relation between ^{0}C and ^{0}F

$$\frac{C}{5} = \frac{F - 32}{9}$$

Relation between ^{0}C and K

$$\boxed{t\,^0C + 273 = TK}$$

Heat energy flows from higher temperature to lower temperature.

Heat (Thermal) capacity [C]: - Amount of heat energy required to raise the temperature of object by 1^0C or 1 K.

$$C' = \frac{\text{Amount of heat energy supplied}}{\text{Rise in temperature}}$$

$$C = \frac{\Delta Q \rightarrow \text{Heat supplied}}{\Delta \theta \rightarrow \text{change in temperature}}$$

Unit of C' is J/^{0}C **or** J/K or Cal / ^{0}C or Cal/ K

Factors affective heat capacity: -

(1) Heat capacity is directly proportional to mass of substance.
(2) Heat capacity depends on material of substance.

Specific heat capacity [c]: -

Amount of heat energy required to raise the temperature of unit substance through 1 ^{0}C or 1K.

"Heat capacity on unit mass is called specific heat capacity".

$$C = \frac{C'}{m} = \frac{\frac{Q}{\Delta\theta}}{m} = \frac{Q}{m\Delta\theta}$$

$$C = \frac{Q}{m\Delta\theta}$$

$\Delta\theta$ = change in temperature

m = mass of substance

Q = amount of heat supplied

Unit of C: - J/kg K or $Jg^{-1}\,{}^0C^{-1}$ or $Jkg^{-1}\,{}^0C^{-1}$ or Cal $kg^{-1}\,{}^0C^{-1}$ or Cal $kg^{-1}\,{}^0k^{-1}$

$$C = \frac{Q}{m\Delta\theta}$$

Q = $mc\Delta\theta$

Measurement of specific heat capacity of object

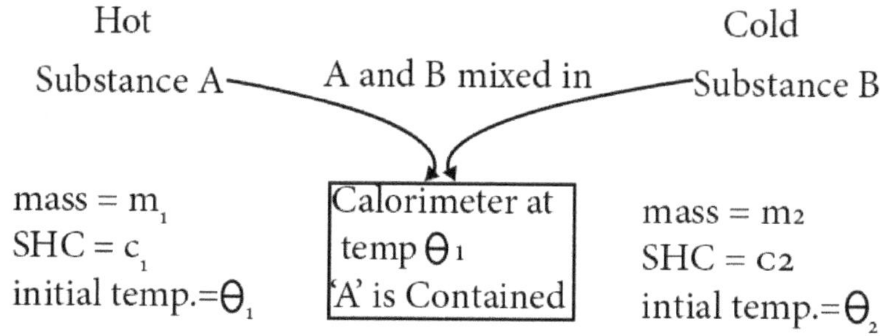

Let final temperature of mixture in θ.

Heat lost by hot body = $m_1C_1(\theta_1 - \theta) + M_{3\ calorimeter}\ C_{3\ calorimeter}(\theta_1 - \theta)$

Heat energy gained by cold body = $m_2 C_2(\theta - \theta_2)$

By Principal of calorimetry

$$\mathbf{m_2c_2(\theta - \theta_2) = m_3c_3(\theta_1 - \theta) + m_1c_1(\theta_1 - \theta)}$$

Measurement of SHC of Liquid: -

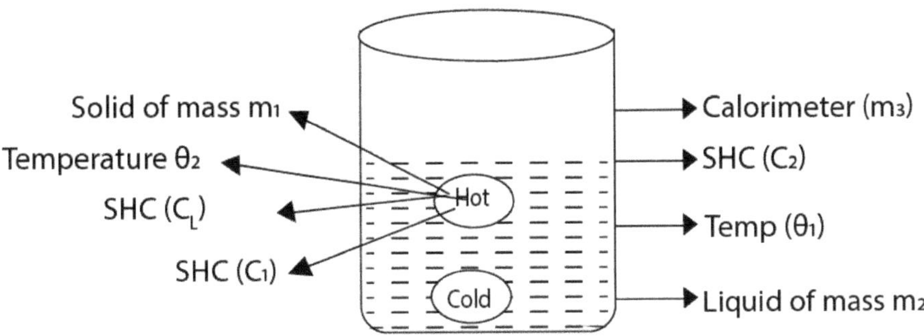

Let final temperature of mixture is θ.
Heat energy last by solid = Heat energy gained by liquid and calorimeter.

$$m_1 c_1 (\theta_2 - \theta) = m_3 c_3 (\theta - \theta_1) + m_2 c_2 (\theta - \theta_1)$$

Change of Phase (State): -

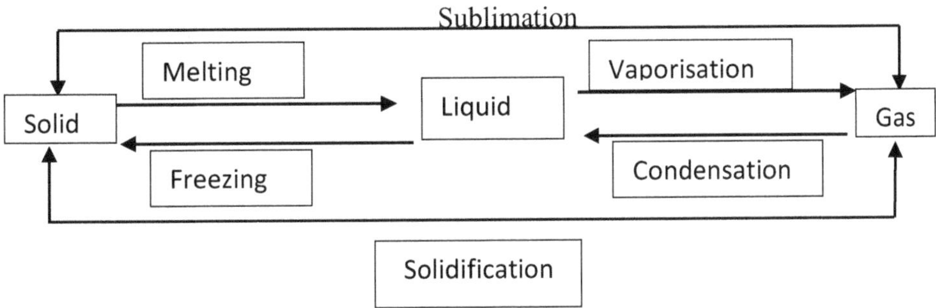

The process of change from one state to another at a constant temperature in called of phase.

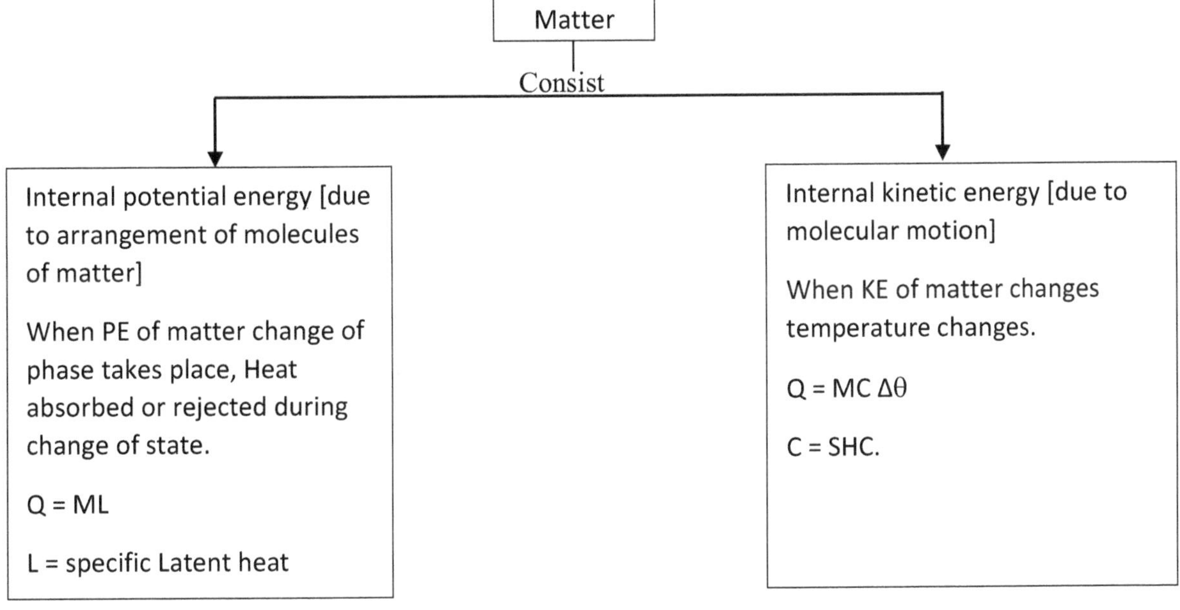

2 ELECTROMAGNETISM

Magnet: - It is an object which attracts substance containing iron, nickel, cobalt etc.

Type of magnet: -

1- Natural magnet
2- Artificial magnet

Magnetic field (B)

The Space around a magnet in which the needle of a compass rests in a direction other than the geographic North – South direction, is called magnetic field of the magnet.

It is a vector quantity, its S.I unit is Tesla (T)

Properties of magnetic field lines: -

1- They are closed and continuous curves.
2- They travel from north pole to south pole outside the magnet, and from South pole to North pole inside the magnet.
3- The tangent at any point on a field line gives the direction of magnetic field at that point.
4- They never intersect each other.
5- They are crowded near the poles of the magnet where the magnetic field is strong and are far separated near the middle of the magnet and for from the magnet where the magnetic field is weak.

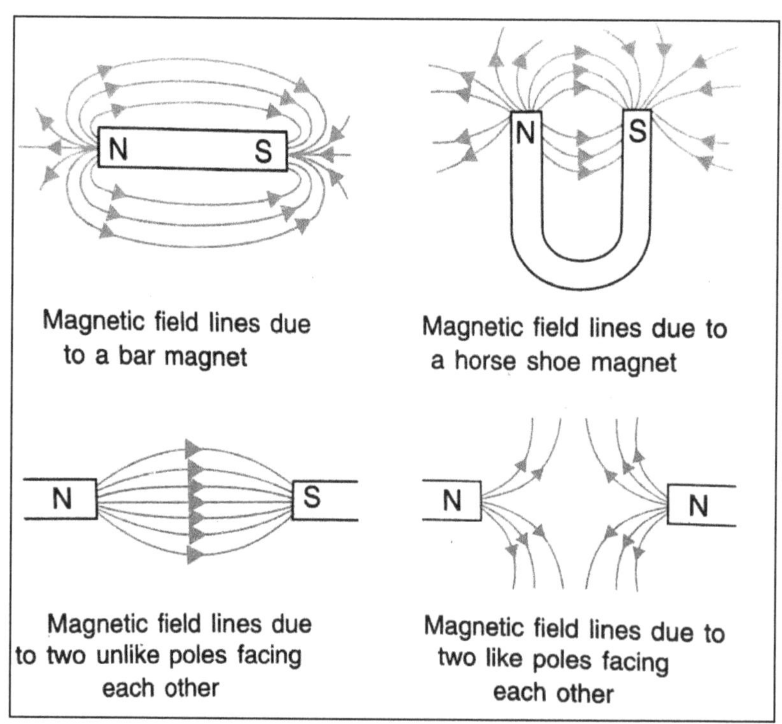

Magnetic field lines due to a bar magnet

Magnetic field lines due to a horse shoe magnet

Magnetic field lines due to two unlike poles facing each other

Magnetic field lines due to two like poles facing each other

Magnetic field lines due to current into straight wire: -

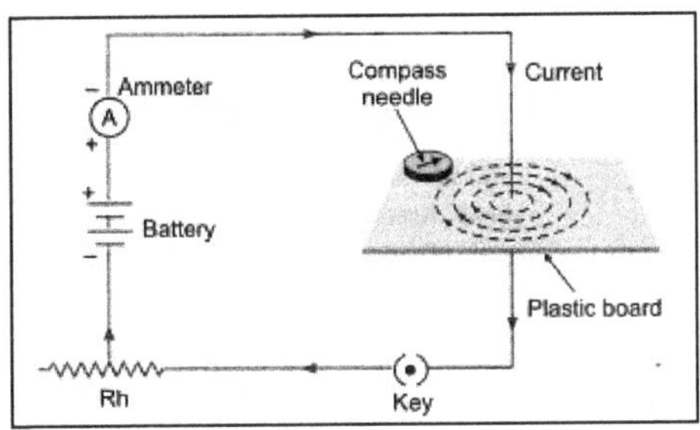

1- The magnetic lines of force are in the form of concentric circles near the conductor.
2- The place of the magnetic lines of force in at right – angles to the straight conductor carrying current.
3- The direction of the magnetic lines of force reverses with the reversal of the direction of current in the conductor.
4- On increasing the strength of current in the conductor, the number of magnetic lines of force around it increases.

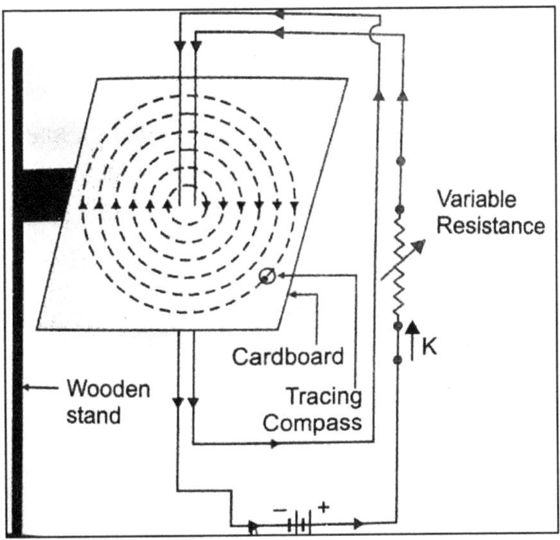

Magnetic field due to current in circular coil:

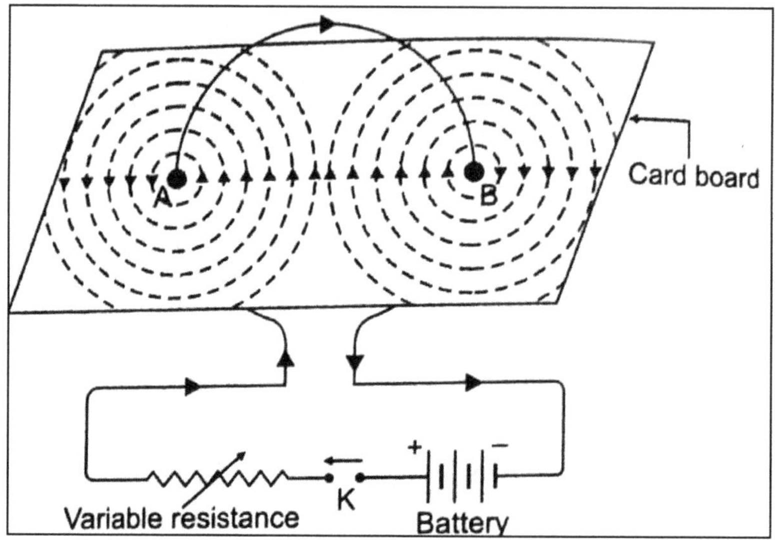

Properties of magnetic lines of force around a circular coil:

1- The magnetic lines of force are near circular at the points, where the enters or leaves the coil.
2- Within the space enclosed by the coil, the lines of force are in the same direction.
3- Near the centre of the coil the magnetic lines of force are almost parallel to each other.
4- At the centre of the coil, the plane of the magnetic lines of force ins at right angles to the plane circular coil.
5- With the increase in the strength of current, the number of magnetic lines of force increase and hence, magnetic intensity increases.

SOLENOID

When insulated copper wire wound on some thin cylindrical card board or plastic tube, such that its length is greater than its diameter and it behaves like a magnet when an electric current is made to flow through it is called a solenoid. Figure 10.13.

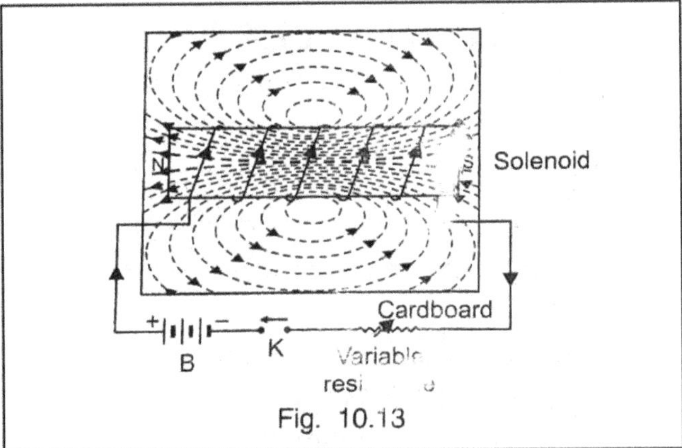

Fig. 10.13

Rule for determining the direction of magnetic lines of force around a conductor carrying current:-

Maxwell's Right Hand Thumb Rule: -

Imagine you holding the conductor with the palm of your right hand, such that the fingers encircle the conductor and the thumb points in the direction of flow of current. Then the direction of the fingers encircling the conductor, gives the direction of the magnetic lines of force around it.

Properties of the solenoid: -

(1) The magnetic field due to solenoid is directly proportional to the number of turns per unit length of the solenoid. $B \propto n$
(2) The magnetic due to the solenoid is directly proportional to the current passing through the solenoid. $B \propto I$
(3) Magnetic fields depend upon the nature of material on which solenoid coil is wound.
(4) When an iron core is inserted inside the solenoid, the magnetic field increases.

Electro magnet:

A solenoid which has an iron core is called an electro magnet.

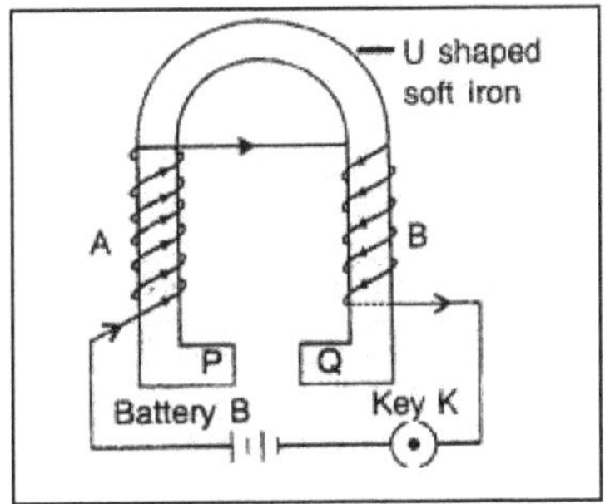

Distinction between an Electromagnet and an Artificial permanent magnet: -

1.	Electromagnet can exhibit much stronger Magnetic field.	Permanent magnet does not exhibit very strong Magnetic field.
2.	The polarity of an electromagnet can be easily reversed by changing the direction of flow of electric current.	The polarity of an artificial or natural magnet is fixed and cannot be reversed easily.
3.	An electromagnet can be easily demagnetised by stopping the current in the solenoid	Artificial or natural magnets cannot be easily de – magnetised.
4.	The strength of the electromagnet can be changed easily by adjusting the magnitude of current.	In case of natural or artificial magnets no such change can be brought about.

Factors determining force acting on a conductor carrying current: -

1- The force is directly proportional to the strength of the current.

$$\text{Force} \propto \text{current}$$

$$F \propto I$$

2- Force experienced by a conductor is directly proportional to the intensity of the magnet field B.

$$F \propto B$$

3- Force experienced by the conductor is directly proportional to the length of the conductor within pole piece of the magnet

$$F \propto L$$

Combining (i) (ii) & (iii)

$$\boxed{F = I.B.L}$$

Fleming's left-hand rule: –

Stretch the thumb, the fore finger and middle finger of your left hand mutually at right angles to each other, such that fore finger point in the direction of the magnetic field and middle finger in direction of the flow of current. Then thumb gives direction of motion of the conductor.

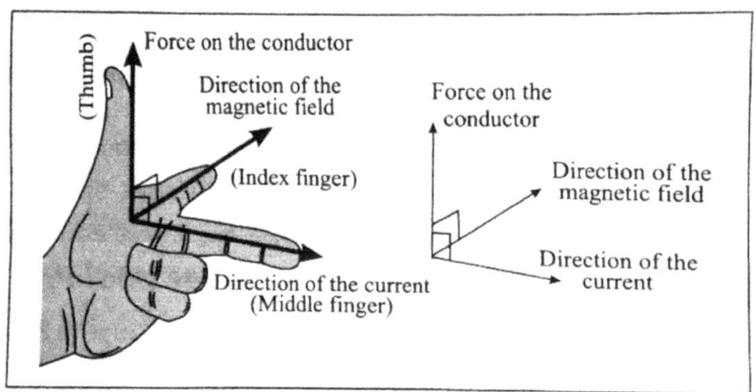

Fleming's left hand rule

D.C motor [Electric motor]: -

A device which convents direct electric current into Mechanical energy is called the D.C motor.

Principle of electric motor: -

When a rectangular coil of many turns and carrying a current is placed in a strong magnetic field, it experiences a torque (couple) and rotates continuously.

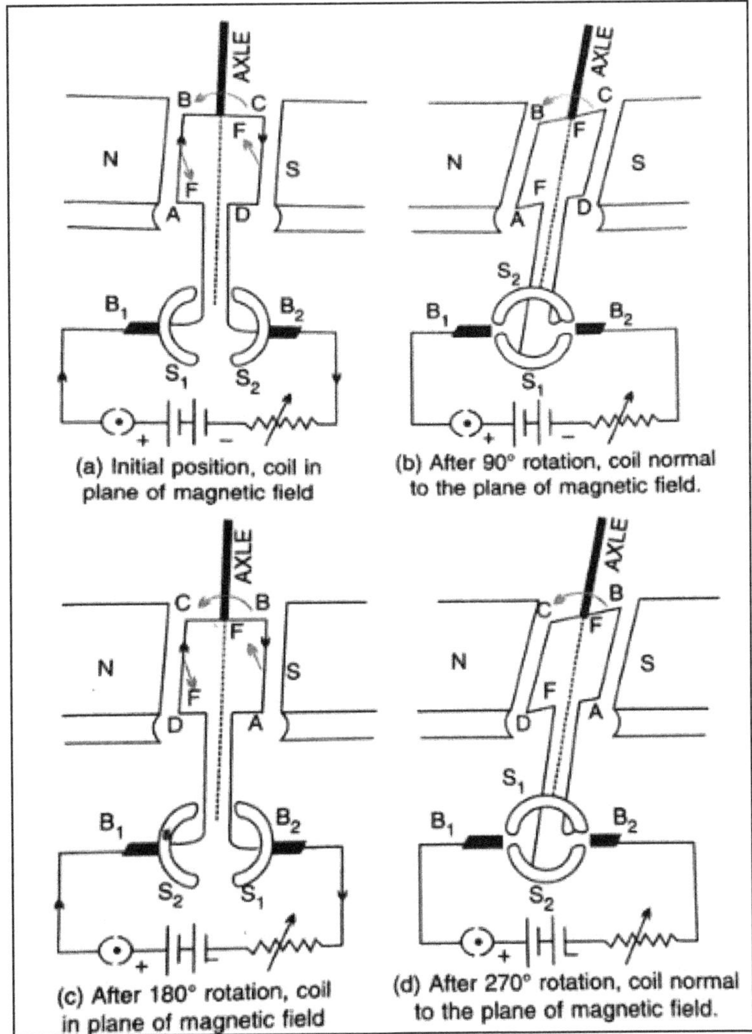

(a) Initial position, coil in plane of magnetic field

(b) After 90° rotation, coil normal to the plane of magnetic field.

(c) After 180° rotation, coil in plane of magnetic field

(d) After 270° rotation, coil normal to the plane of magnetic field.

Electromagnetic induction: -

Electromagnetic induction is the phenomenon in which e.m.f is induced in the coil if there is a change in the magnetic flux linked with the coil.

Faraday's laws of electromagnetic induction: -

1- Whenever there is a change in the magnetic flux lined with a coil, an e.m.f is induced.

2- The magnitude of the e.m.f induced is directly proportional to the rate of change of the magnetic flux linked with the coil.

Factor affecting the magnitude of induced E.M.F: -

1- The change in the magnetic flux.
2- The time in which the magnetic flux changes.

Direction of induced E.M.F: -

1- Fleming's Right-hand rule: -

Stretch the thumb, the forefinger and the middle finger of your right hand mutually at right angles to each other, such that the forefinger points in the direction of the magnetic field and the thumb in the direction in which the middle finger points, gives the direction of the flow of the induced current.

2- Lenz's Law: -
It states that the direction of induced E.M.F. always tends to oppose the cause which produces it.

A.C. Generator: -

An A.C generator in a device which converts the Mechanical energy into the electrical energy.

Principal: - Electromagnetic induction.

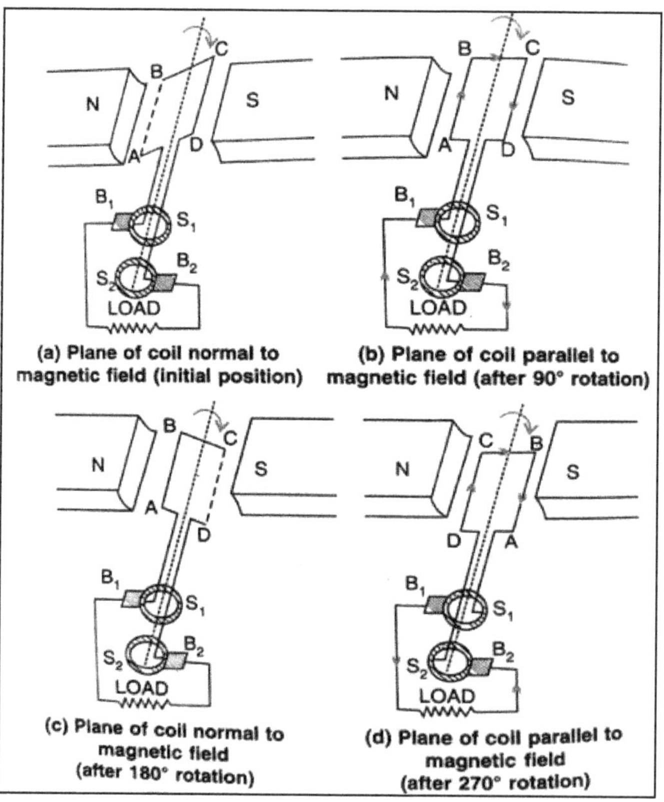

Transformer: -Transformer is a device by which the amplitude of an alternating E.M.F can be increased or decreased.

Principle: - Electromagnetic induction.

Type of Transformer

1- Step – up transformer
2- Step- down transformer

Turns Ratio ' n ' = $\frac{\text{Number of turn in secondary coil (Ns)}}{\text{Number of turn in primary coil (Np)}}$

$$\frac{Es}{Ep} = \frac{Ns}{Np} = \text{Turn ratio 'n'}$$

Where Es = E.M.F across the secondary coil.

Ep = E.M.F across the primary coil.

Ns = number of turns on secondary coil.

Np = number of turns in primary coil.

3 CURRENT ELECTRICITY

Electricity is a branch of physics in which we deal with the property of charges at rest or in motion.

Charge (Q or q): - It is the fundamental property of matter other than mass which creates electric forces.

S.I unit of charge ⟶ Coulomb's (C)
C.G.S unit of charge ⟶ State – Coulomb's (st - c)
Or
Franklin (Fr)

Type of charge

1. **Positive charge**
2. **Negative charge**

Quantization of charge = **$Q = ne$** **where** Q = charge

n = number of free electrons

e^- = charge on an electron

Properties of charge

1. Like charges repel each other.
2. Unlike charge attracts each other.
3. Law of conservation of charge = According to this charge can neither be created nor it can be destroyed, it can be transferred from one body to another body by friction, conduction & induction.

Current = **(I)** Rate of flow of charge is called current.

- The S.I unit of current is ampere (A)
- It is a scalar quantity.

$$I = \frac{Q}{t} = \frac{ne}{t}$$

Q = Charge

I = Current

t = Time

- One Ampere ⟶ Rate of flow of one coulomb Charge in one second is Called one ampere.

- Other units of current

  $1A = \frac{1C}{1s}$

- 1 mA = 10^{-3}A

  1 mA = 10^{-6}A

  1 mA = 10^{3}A

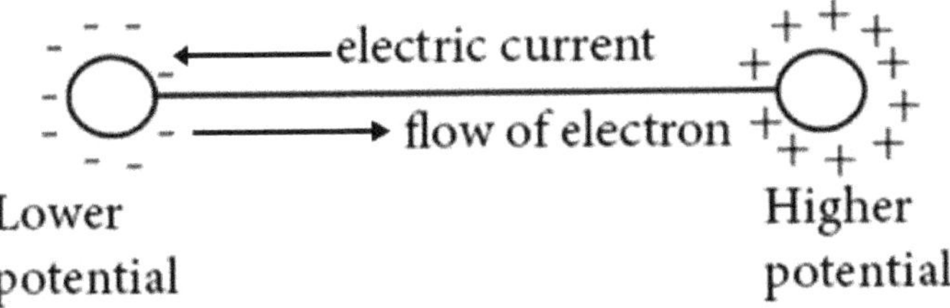

Electrostatic potential: -

The stamina to conduct the charge from one object to another object it is measured by work done.

Potential difference (P.d or V): -

It is numerically equal to work done in bringing unit positive charge from point to another point.

- It is a scalar quantity.
- It S.I unit is volt or J/C

$\{V = \frac{W}{q}\}$ where, V = Potential difference

w = Work done

q = charge

Electric Potential: -

It is numerically equal to work done in bringing unit positive charge from infinity to a particular point.

- It is a Scalar quantity
- It S.I unit is volt or J/C

Direction of current: -

Electronic current ⇒ -ive terminal to +ive terminal.

Conventional current ⇒ +ive terminal to -ive terminal.

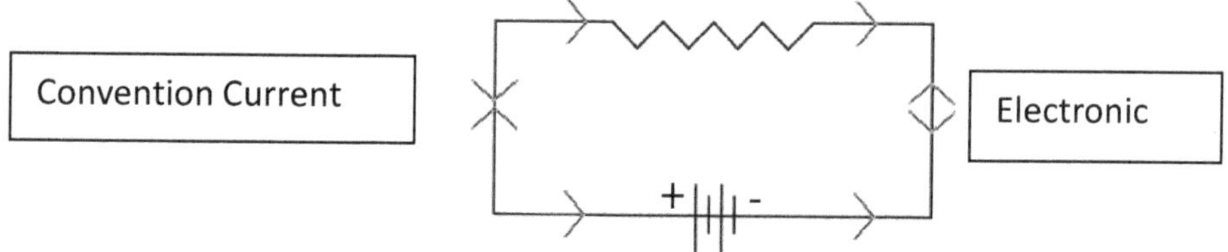

Resistance (R)

The obstruction offered to electric current through conductor is called electric Resistance.

- It is a scalar is quantity.
- Its S.I unit is ohm (Ω)

$$R = \frac{V}{I}$$

Where, R = Resistance
V = Potential difference
I = Current

Factor affecting the Resistance: -

1- Resistance is directly proportional to its length (L)

$$R \propto L \text{ ——————— } (1)$$

2- Resistance is inversely proportional to its Area of cross – section (A)

$$R \propto \frac{1}{A} \text{ ——————— } (2)$$

3- Nature of Conductor.
4- Resistance of conductor increase with increase in temperature.

Specific Resistance (Resistivity)

1- $R \propto L$ ——————— (1)
2- $R \propto \frac{1}{A}$ ——————— (2)

Join (1) & (2)

$$R \propto \frac{1}{A}$$

$$R = \rho\frac{l}{A}$$

Where, R = Resistance
ρ = Resistivity
L = Length of conductor
A = Area of cross - section

[ρ is constant called Resistivity]

$$\rho = \frac{\mathbf{R \cdot A}}{\mathbf{l}}$$

Resistivity is equal to Resistance of 1m long wire whose area of cross – section is $1m^2$.

- its S.I unit is Ohm-meter $(\Omega - m)$

- Resistivity depends upon temperature & Nature Conductor.

Ohm's law

Al constant Physical factor (Length, area of cross-section, temperature) potential difference across the conductor is directly proportional to amount of current flowing through the conductor.

$V \propto I$

Or

$I \propto V$

$V = R I$

V – I graph +

Basic Electrical Circuit (Diagram)

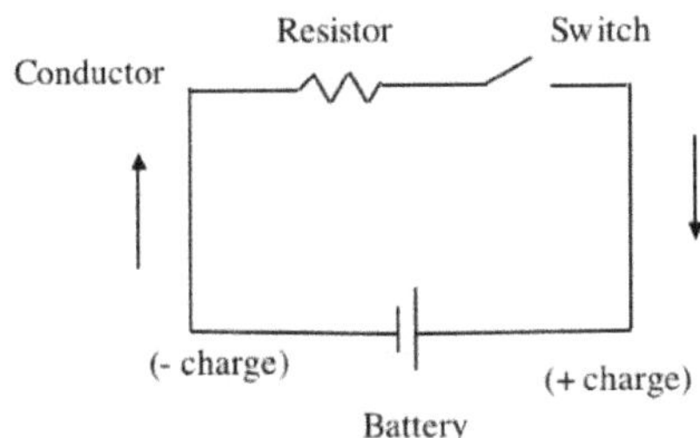

$$\text{Slope} = \frac{y_2 - y_1}{x_2 - x_1}$$

$$R = \frac{\Delta V}{\Delta I}$$

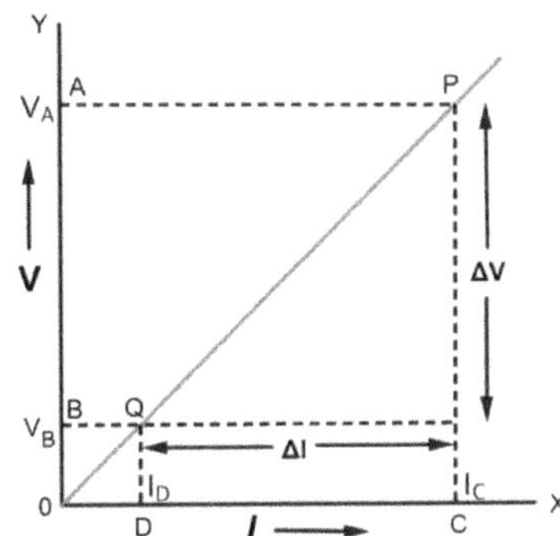

Ohmic & Non- Ohmic Resistor: -

- **Ohmic Resistor: -**

The conductor which obeys ohm's law are called ohmic conductors or Resistors.

Ex. All metals etc.

- **Non – Ohmic Resistor: -**

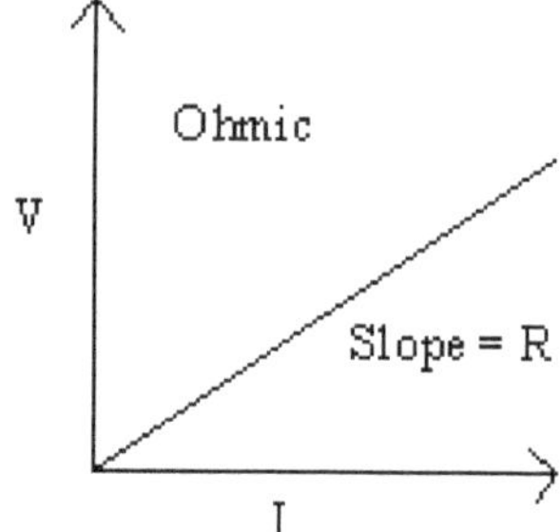

The conductor which does not obey ohm's law are called as Non – ohmic conductors.

Ex. Semi-conductor diode, triode etc.

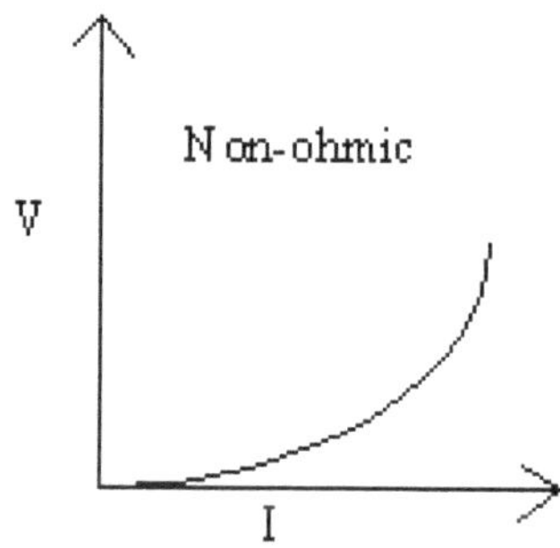

1. **Conductance (G): -**

   Reciprocal of Resistance is known as conductance.

   $$G = \frac{1}{\text{Resistance}}$$

   Its S.I unit is (Ω^{-1}) or Siemen

2. **Conductivity (σ): -**
   The reciprocal of Resistivity is known as conductivity. It represented by the symbol σ (sigma).

   $$\sigma = \frac{1}{\rho} = \frac{L}{RA}$$

   Its S.I unit is ($\Omega^{-1}m^{-1}$) or Siemen meter $^{-1}$

Cell: - Cell is a device which is used to convert chemical energy to electrical energy.

Two types of cells

1- Primary cell

2- Secondary cell

Terms Related to cell

1- **Electro – motive force (E.M.F.) of cell: -**

When no current is drawn from the cell then potential difference between the terminal of cell is called E.M.F.

- Its S.I unit is Volt (V)

2- **Terminal potential difference (Terminal Voltage(V)**

When current is drawn from the cell than the Potential difference between the terminal of cell is called terminal voltage.

- Its S.I unit is volt (V)

$$V = I R$$

3- **Internal Resistance (r)**

Obstruction offered by electrolyte in flow of electron is called internal Resistance

Its S.I unit is ohm.

$$R = \frac{V}{I}$$

4- **Voltage drops – (V)**

It is the product of current drown from the cell and internal Resistance of cell.

$$V = I.\ r$$

Relationship between E.M.F Terminal voltage & internal Resistance of cell: -

$E = V + v$

$E = IR + I\,r$

$$E = I\,(R + r)$$

$$V = IR$$
$$V = I\,r$$

Factor affecting the internal Resistance: -

1- Internal Resistance is directly proportional to concentration of electrolyte.
2- Internal Resistance is inversely proportional to surface area of electrode.
3- Internal Resistance is directly proportional to distance between the terminal of cell.
4- Internal Resistance depend on temperature of the electrolyte.

Combination of Resistance: -

1- Series Resistance
2- Parallel Resistance
3- Both in series & parallel

1. **Series combination of Resistance: -**

* In series combination current will be same in each of Resistor.
* In series combination potential difference will be different in each of Resistor.

Equivalent Resistance: -

$$R_{eq} = R_1 + R_2 + R_3 \text{--------------------}$$

- If 'n' Resistors are connected

$$R_{eq} = R_1 + R_2 + R_3 \text{--------------------} R_n$$

2- **Parallel combination of Resistance: -**

- In Parallel combination potential difference will be same across each resister.
- In Parallel combination current will be different in each resistor.

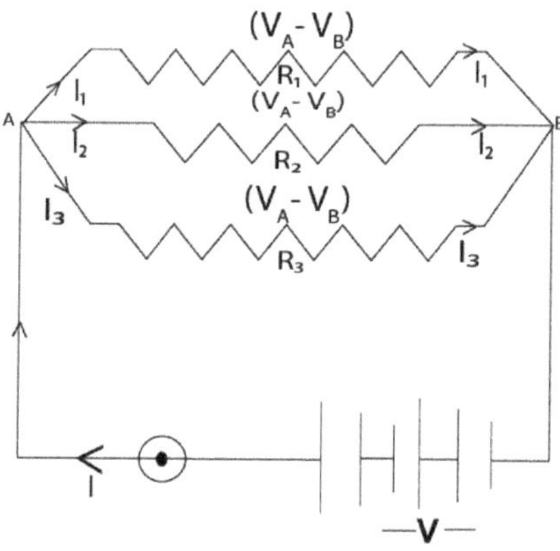

- Equivalent Resistance

- If n conductors are in parallel

$$\frac{1}{R_{eq}} = \frac{1}{R_1} + \frac{1}{R_2} + \frac{1}{R_3} + \dots\dots\dots + \frac{1}{R_n}$$

Electric power & Household Circuits: -

Electrical energy: - the capacity to do electrical work is called Electric Energy.

- Symbol E(w)
- S.I unit Joule (J)
- C.G.S unit erg
- 1 Joule = 10^7 erg

Other Units: -

1electron Volt (ev) = 1.6×10^{-19} joule

1 Mega electron volt (Mev) = 1.6×10^{-13} Joule

1 Calorie = 4.2Joule.

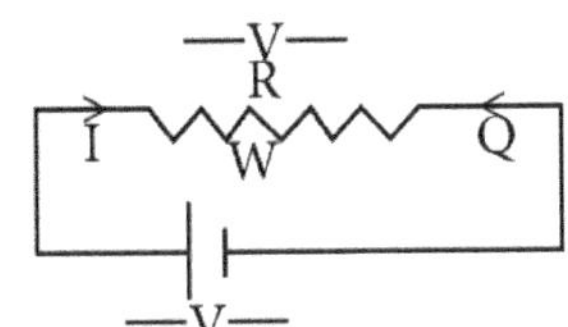

Electrical Energy = Work done by the charge against Resistance of load.

$V = \frac{W}{Q}$ 　　 $V = IR$

$Q = It$

$W = VQ$

$W = IR.\ It$

$W = I^2Rt$

$W = I^2\ R.\ t$

$\boxed{E = I^2 R t}$ $\{I = \frac{V}{R}\}$

$E = \frac{V^2}{R} t$

Where – E = Electrical energy

V = Potential difference

R = Resistance

t = Time.

Electric Power: - Rate of doing electric work is called electric power.

$$\text{Power} = \frac{\text{work}}{\text{time}}$$

$$\text{Power} = \frac{VIT}{t} \qquad \{W = VIt\}$$

It is Scalar quantity.

$P = V.\ I$

V = Potential difference

I = Current

$P = I^2\ R$

$$P = \frac{V^2}{R}$$

- Its S.I unit is watt or (J / s)

1 Watt: - One watt in the electric power consumed when 1 joule of work is done 1 second.

Other Unit:

1 kilowatt (1kW) = 1000 W

1 Megawatt (1MW) = 10^6W

Commercial Unit of Electrical Energy: -

Kilowatt – hour (kWh)

Watt –hour (Wh)

1 Watt hour = 3600 J

1 Kilowatt hour = 3.6×10^6 J

$$\boldsymbol{Energy\ (kWh) = \frac{Power\ (W) x\ time\ (h)}{1000}}$$

$$\boldsymbol{Energy\ (kWh) = \frac{V(Volt) x I\ (ampere) x\ time\ (h)}{1000}}$$

House hold consumption of electrical energy: -

Energy (in kWh) = Power (kW) x time (h)

Heating effect of current: -

$$H = I^2 R t$$

Where, H = Heat

I = Current

R = Resistance

t = Time

Factor affecting Heating effect of current: -

1- Amount of current
$$H \propto I^2$$
2- The Resistance of wire
$$H \propto R$$

3- The time for which current is passed in the wire.

$$H \propto t$$

It is also known as "Joule's law of Heating"

Power Distribution in a House: -

1- Tree System.
2- Ring System.

Ring system: -

Advantage: -

- All device and loads are connected in parallel.
- For new installation in rooms, we don't need further wiring from distribution box.
- At the time of wiring, it is expensive but in future we can install any device of any current carrying capacity.

Tree System Disadvantage: -

- In this if we install a new electrical device in a particular room, we have to make a new line (Live wise) supply from distribution box which is expensive.
- Sometimes is this system rooms are connected in series which is wrong.

Switches: -

A switch is an on – off device for making or breaking of an electrical circuit. A switch is connected in the live wire of the electric circuit.

Types of switches: -

(1) Single pole switch.
(2) Dual pole switch or staircase switch.

Three pin plugs

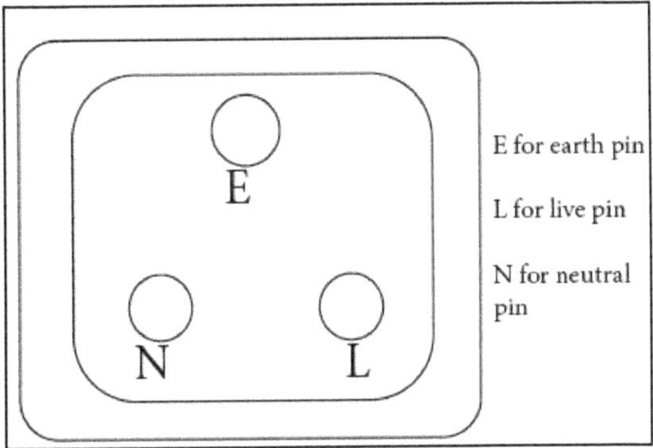

Colour coding of wire in a cable

Wire	Colour Code.	
	Old Convention	**New Convention**
Live (L)	Red	Brown
Neutral (N)	Black	Light blue
Earth (E)	Green	Green or yellow

4 SOUND

Sound is a form of energy which causes a sensation of Hearing.

Cause: - Sound is produced by vibration.

Vibration: - One complete to and from or up and down motion is known as vibration.

Type of sound

(i) **Infra sonic sound: -** The sound having frequency less than 20 Hz is called infrasonic sound.
(ii) **Audible sound: -** The sound having frequency 20 Hz to 20,000 Hz.
(iii) **Ultra-sonic sound: -** Sound having frequency more than 20,000 Hz (20kHz).

Natural time period: - The time period of a body executing natural vibration is called Natural time period.

Free or Natural Vibration: -

The Vibration produced in a body on being slightly disturbed from its mean position are called free vibration.

Damped Vibration

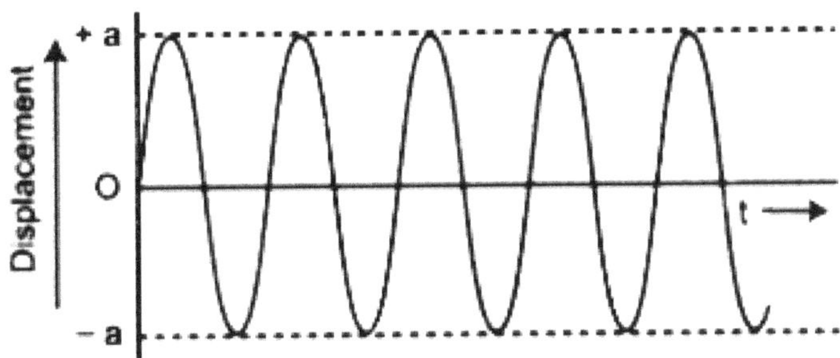

The periodic vibration of continuously decreasing amplitude is called damped vibration.

Ex. 1- Vibration of a tuning for in air.
2- Vibration of stringed instrument in air.
3- Vibration of a simple pendulum in air.

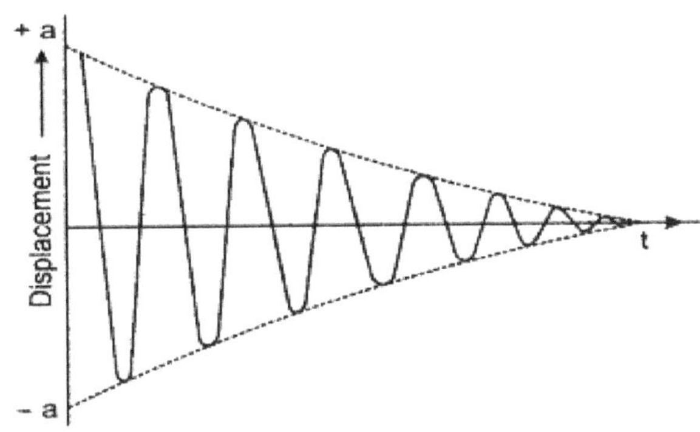

Forced Vibration

The vibration which takes place under the influence of an external periodic forced are called forced vibration.

Ex.1- When the handle of a vibrating tuning fork is pressed against a table top, a loud sound is heard.

2- When the wire of a sitar or a guitar is plucked, its board and wind box make forced vibration.

Resonance: -

It is defined as a phenomenon, when the frequency of an applied external force is equal to the natural frequency of the body on which the force is applied, such that it easily takes up the vibration and begins to vibrate with an increased amplitude.

Condition for the phenomenon of Resonance: -

1- The Natural frequency of the given body must be equal to the frequency of the vibration body.
2- The vibrating body must have sufficient force, so as to set the other body into vibrations.

Examples of Resonance: -

1. It is a common experience that the frame of a motor cycle vibrates violently when driven at some particular speed. The reason is that at the particular speed the natural frequency of the frame matches with that of the piston of the engine, and hence, resonance takes place. It is on account of the same reason that a particular railway compartment makes a lot of noise, even when the train is moving in an open countryside.
2. Sometimes a wire glass or any odd piece of cutlery starts vibrating, when a particular note is struck, because its natural frequency matches with that of the impressed frequency of the note.
3. Tuning forks are often mounted on sound boxes. The size and the amount of air enclosed in the sound box is so adjusted that its natural frequency matches with the frequency of the tuning fork, and hence, a loud sound is produced due to resonance.
4. Soldiers are often asked to break their steps while crossing a bridge. This precaution is taken to prevent any sudden collapse of the bridge, due to matching of the natural frequency of the bridge with that of the impressed force due to the marching of soldiers.
5. Certain toys are so constructed that their diaphragm starts vibrating in resonance with some particular notes from a whistle. In such cases, when a whistle is blown the vibration in the diaphragm makes the toy work.
6. Resonance is not only confined to sound waves, but takes place in electromagnetic waves, such as.

Characteristics of sound: -

(1) Loudness

(2) pitch (or shrillness)

(3) quality (or timbre)

Loudness OR Intensity

Intensity of sound is the time rate at which the sound Energy flows through a Unit area.

* Intensity and loudness are not the same.

* Intensity depends on the energy per unit area of the waves.

$$I = \frac{E}{A.t}$$

Where, I = Intensity

E = Energy

A = Unit area

t = time

Its S.I unit is $= \frac{\text{Joule}}{\text{Meter2.Second}}$ or J/m^2. S

* The Subjective property of sound by virtue of which a person can distinguish a louder & a faint sound.
* Loudness is a feeling it can be measured by intensity.
* Loudness is measured in db (decibel) or phon.
* Sound whose loudness more than 120 dB is known as noise.

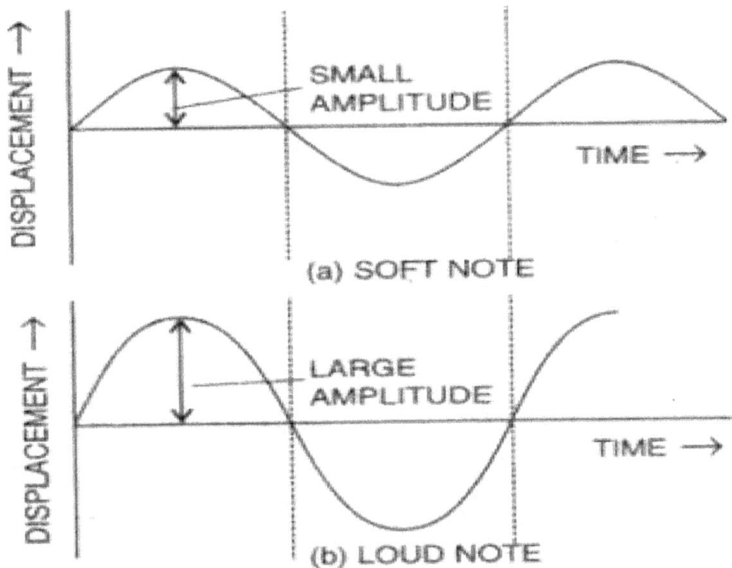

(a) SOFT NOTE

(b) LOUD NOTE

Factors affecting the loudness: -

i) Loudness is directly proportional to surface area of vibrating medium.
ii) Loudness is directly proportional to square of amplitude.
iii) In the presence of resonant body loudness of sound of increases.
iv) Loudness is inversely proportional to square of distance.
v) Loudness is directly proportional. Temperature of medium.

Pitch: - The Subjective property of sound due to which a person can distinguish Between a shrill note and a flat note of same loudness and same quality.

- Pitch of a note depends on its frequency.

- The wavelength of a sound wave varies inversely as its frequency. It has the same relationship with the pitch also.

Quality (Timbre): -

The notes of different instruments having the same frequencies and same loudness are distinguished by this characteristic.

- Sound produced by different musical instruments differ in:
  (a) Wavelength
  (b) Loudness
  (c) Wave form

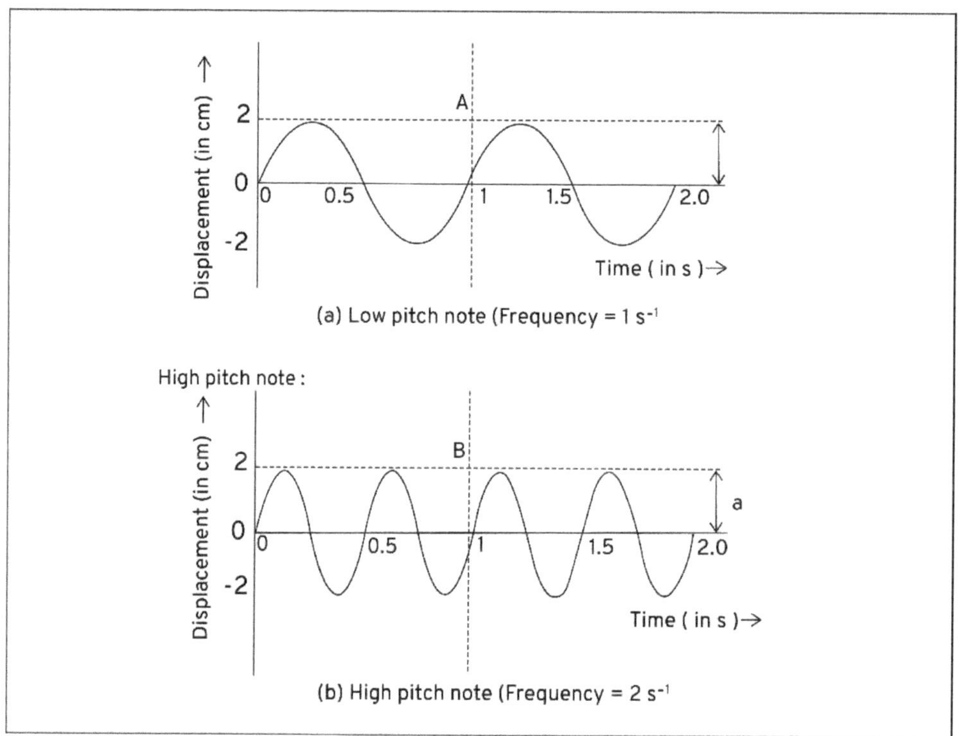

(a) Low pitch note (Frequency = 1 s^{-1}

(b) High pitch note (Frequency = 2 s^{-1}

- The quality of a note depends on the wave form.

Musical Sound: - Sound waves which produce pleasant sensation in our ears and are acceptable are known as musical sound.

Noise: - Sound waves which produce troublesome sensation and are unacceptable are known as noise.

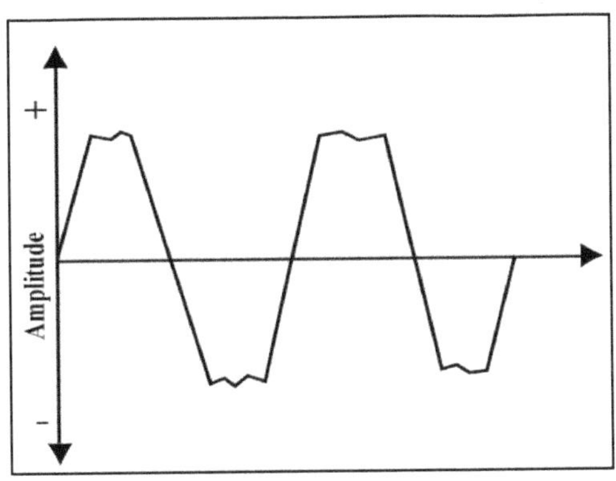
+
Amplitude
-

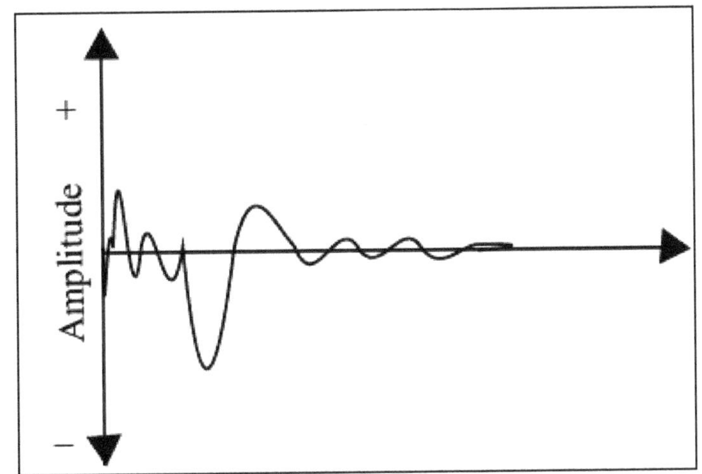
+
Amplitude
–

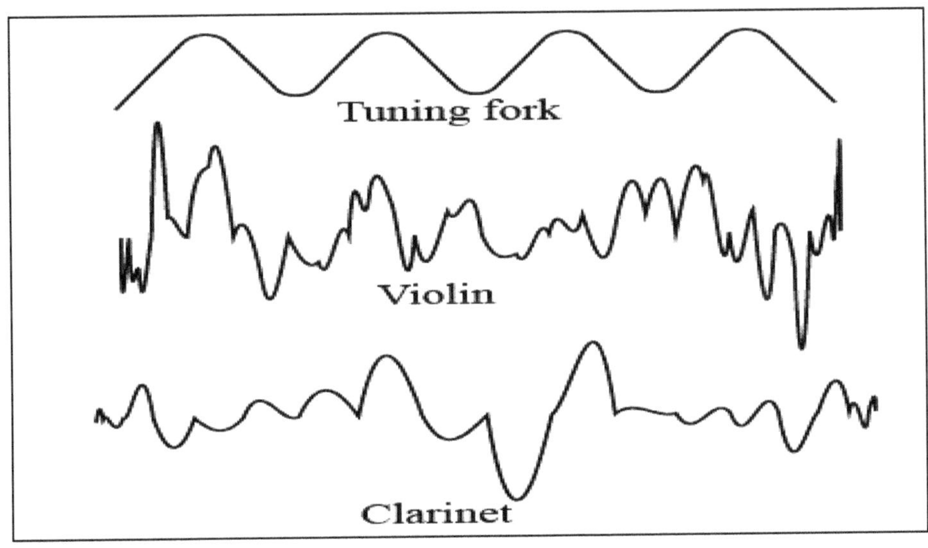
Tuning fork
Violin
Clarinet

5 RADIOACTIVITY

Radioactivity: - It is the process of Spontaneous decay of unstable nuclei emitting α or β particle and γ rays from the Nucleus of atoms.

Atomic Number: - (Z) The atomic number of an atom is the number of protons in its nucleus.

(Which is the same as the number of electrons in a neutral atom)

Mass Number (A): - The sum of total number of protons and neutrons inside the atomic nucleus of the element is known as its mass number.

* The term "nucleon" is also used for neutron and proton

Isotopes: - The atoms of some elements having same number of protons but different number of neutrons are called isotopes.

Ex. $_1H^1$, $_1H^2$, $_1H^3$ etc.

Isobars: - The atoms of different elements having the same mass number (A) but different atomic number (Z) are called isobars.

Ex. $_{11}Na^{23}$, and $_{12}Mg^{23}$, are isobars.

Isotones: - The atoms having different number of protons but same number of neutrons are called isotones.

Ex. $_{19}K^{39}$ and $_{20}C^{40}$

$_3Li^7$ and $_4Be^8$ etc.

CHARACTERISTICS OF ALPHA RAYS (i.e., α-PARTICLES)

(i) Alpha rays consist of stream of positively charged particles carrying charge of $+2$ units and a mass of four units on the atomic weight scale (i.e., 4 a.m.u.). In other words, these particles are helium nuclei and therefore indicated as $_2He^4$ or $_2\alpha^4$.

(ii) They affect photographic plate.

(iii) They are deflected only slightly towards the negative plate in electric field. They are also deflected by magnetic field.

(iv) These particles when passed through gases produce ionisation in them. Alpha particles have maximum ionising power.

(v) They have a velocity of the order of $1 \times 10^7 ms^{-1}$.

(vi) They have very little penetrating power.

(vii) By emission of an α-particle, atomic number of nucleus decreases by 2 units and mass number by 4 units.

CHARACTERISTICS OF BETA RAYS (i.e., β -PARTICLES)

(i) Beta rays are made up of streams of negatively charged particles similar to electrons. Thus, β-particle has a unit negative charge and a negligible mass. Hence, β-particle is represented as -1 β0.
(ii) They affect photographic plate.
(iii) They get deflected to the maximum extent towards the positive plate in electric field.
(iv) They are also deflected by 'magnetic field.
(v) Their ionising power is less than that of β-rays. (It is about one hundredth of α-particles).
(vi) Their velocity varies with the source but is nearing the velocity of light.
(vii) Their penetration power is about 100 times more than that of α-particles.
(viii) By emission of a β-particle, atomic number of nuclei increases by one whereas mass

CHARACTERISTICS OF GAMMA (γ) RAYS

1. They are electromagnetic radiation like X- rays having very short wavelength, in the range of 10^{-10} m to 10^{-13} m.
2. They effect photographic plate.
3. They are unaffected by electric and magnetic fields.
4. Their ionising power is low, (about one hundredth of β-particles).
5. Their Velocity is same as that of light.
6. Their penetrating power is very high, about 100 times more than that of β-particles. Hence, they are also called as hard rays.
7. When α and β particles are emitted by in atom, there is always a re-arrangement in the nucleus and during this process some energy is given out in the form of γ-rays.
   Thus, emission of gamma rays accompanies virtually all nuclear reactions

SI.NO.	α- particles	β-particles	γ-radiation
1.	α- particles is the helium nucleus ($_2He^4$)	α- particles is nothing but like an electron ($_{-1}e^0$).	γ-rays are electromagnetic Radiations.
2.	It is +vely charged	It is –vely charged	It is no charge.
3.	The mass of each α-particle is 4 a.m.u. about 1/1836 a.m.u.	The mass of each β-particle is negligible.	It is no mass
4	Its velocity is less than the velocity of light, about 1-2 x 10^7 m/s.	Its velocity is less than the velocity of light but not very less than it.	Its velocity is the same as that of light.

5.	Its ionisation power is the max. It is about 100 times more than that a β-particles.	Its ionisation power is about 100 times more than that of γ-rays.	The ionisation power is the least.
6.	The penetrating power is the least.	Penetrating power is less but 100 times more than penetrating power of α-particles.	Penetrating power maximum i.e., 100 of β-particles.
7.	Less defected by electric and magnetic fields.	More deflected in a direction opposite to alpha particles by electric and magnetic fields.	They are unaffected by electric and magnetic fields.

Some radioactive decays are as follows.

* **α- Decay: -** In α- decay the mass number of the daughter nucleus is four less than that of parent nucleus, while atomic number decreases by two.

$$ {}^{A}_{Z}X \longrightarrow {}^{A-4}_{Z-2}Y + {}^{4}_{2}He $$

(Parent nucleus) (Doughter nucleus) (α- particles)

Ex. ${}_{92}U^{238} \longrightarrow {}_{90}Th^{234} + {}_{2}He^{4}$

* **β-Decay: -** The mass number of the daughter nucleus remains same but atomic number increases by one.

$$ {}^{A}_{Z}X \longrightarrow {}^{A}_{Z+1}X + \beta^{-} ({}_{1}e^{0}) $$

Ex. ${}_{6}C^{14} \longrightarrow {}_{7}N^{14} + {}_{-1}e^{0}$

* **Gamma Decay: -** In γ- Decay there is no change in mass number and atomic number of electromagnetic radiations is related this decay.

(Parent nucleus) (Doughter nucleus) (gamma radiation or energy)

Uses of Radioactive isotopes: -

In Medicine

Radioisotopes are used in detection of diseases and also in radio therapy.

a) the rays from radium produce satisfactory improvement in skin diseases.
b) Radiation from Co^{60} (γ- rays) is used in cancer treatment.
c) Radio iodine (I^{131}) is used to diagnose and treat thyroid disorders.
d) Radio phosphorus (P^{32}) is used the treatment of leukaemia and tumours.
e) Radio sodium (Na^{24}) in the form of $NaCl$ is used to study the circulation of blood.

In Agriculture

(a) Radioactive phosphorus (P^{32}) is used in the study of metabolism of plants.

(b) Radioactive sulphur (S^{35}) helps to study advantages and disadvantages of fungicides.

(c) Pests and insects on crops can be killed by γ-radiations.

(d) γ-rays are used for preservation of milk, potatoes etc.

(e) Field of crops like carrot, root, apples, grapes can be increased by irradiation with radioisotopes.

In Industry

(a) In manufacturing paper, plastic and metal sheets to control the thickness of the sheets.

(b) Radioisotopes can be used to estimate the amount of wear in bearings.

(c) Leaks in pipes may be traced by introducing a small quantity of a radioisotope into the fluid in the pipe.

(d) It is also used to detect the cracks in the welding, casting, etc.

Background radiation: -

The low temperature microwave radiation that arrives at the earth's surface from all directions of outer space is called background radiation. It is so named because it forms a background to all the radio sources that have been detected by radio telescopes. Cosmic background radiation was predicted to exist as part of the Big Bang theory of the origin of the universe. According to this theory such radiation is the lingering prevailed in the first moment of the Big Bang.
A number of sources other than the cosmic radiation from the space contribute to the background radiation.
These may be:

(a) Radiation from the sun.

(b) Rocks in the earth which contain traces of radioactive substances.

(c) Naturally occurring radioisotopes/radar.

(d) Artificial radioisotopes.

(e) Products made from nuclear explosions, e.g., strontium-90 which has a half-life of 28 years.

(f) *X*-rays is high frequency, highly penetrating electromagnetic radiation produced when high energy electron hits heavy metal target. Recent researches show that wavelength of continuous spectrum of X-ray is less than that of gamma radiation from radioactive sources. Use of one background radiation received for 10 days.

(g) Potassium and carbon from human body.

(h) Radiations from self-luminous dials.

Hazards and Safety Measures of Radiations: -

Dangers of Radiation

Some of the damage caused by the emitted radiation became evident within days, but some did not become evident until years after the event. Some of the effects on humans of exposure to large doses or prolonged small doses of radiation, mostly y-radiation. Are

i) Burns

ii) Leukaemia (cancer of the blood), eve cataracts

iii) Sterility (inability to produce children)

iv) Some children born with serious abnormalities as their genes get damaged

v) Damage to the blood may lower resistance to dangerous because of their high penetrating they are used.

vi) Radioisotopes increase the level of radiation but the effects can be minimized by using there with a fairly short half-life. This Perion should the long enough to do what is required. but short

vii) normal diseases

Nuclear fission

Safety Precautions

The growth and use of radioactive product has increased considerably since about 1930. Radioactive sources have become part of normal school equipment and although the sources are very weak, it is essential to take stringent safety precautions. The following precautions are to be taken:

- **i.** The sources should only be handled by the forceps provided and never touched by hand.
- **ii.** They should never be pointed towards a person.
- **iii.** Food should not be taken where the sources are being used, because it may become contaminated.
- **iv.** Never smoke near a radioactive source.
- **v.** The user should wear rubber gloves, and hands should be washed after the sources have been put away safely:
- **vi.** In places where the quantities of radioactive materials used are greater, special clothing is worn and photographic emulsions or some means of monitoring the radiation are used. α-particles cause intense ionization but they are easily absorbed by protective clothing. Thus. they are not likely to do much damage unless they enter the body on contaminated food etcβ-particles have a greater range, but they too are easily absorbed, and a Perspex screen may be used as protection. y-rays are most nuclear fission is the process of splitting of a happy nucleus into two or more light nuclei releasing tremendous amount of energy fission of uranium is represented by the following equation.

$$9_2U^{235} + {}_0n^1 \longrightarrow 9_2U^{236} \longrightarrow {}_{56}a^{144} + {}^{15r^{89}}_{36} + 8_0n^1 + 200\text{ MeV}$$

Nuclear Fusion:

Nuclear fusion is a process in which two light nuclei combine to form a heavy nucleus but is not possible at ordinary temperature and pressure fusion equation for two deuterium nuclei is.

$$\overset{H^2}{1} + {}_1H^2 \longrightarrow {}_1H^3 + {}_1H^1 + 4M_{eV}$$

DISTINCTION BETWEEN THE NUCLEAR FISSION AND NUCLEAR FUSION

Nuclear fission	Nuclear fusion
1) In fission when neutrons are bombarded on a heavy nucleus, it splits in two nearly equal light fragments. 2) This reaction is possible at ordinary temperature and ordinary pressure. 3) In one fission reaction nearly $190MeV$ energy is released. 4) For the same mass, the energy released in the fission process is less than that in the fusion process. 5) The fissionable substance is radioactive, so it gives out the harmful radiations and it creates problem in disposal of its waste.	1) In fusion, at a very high temperature and high pressure two light nuclei combine to form a heavy nucleus. 2) This reaction is possible only at a very high temperature $(= 10^7K)$ and a very high pressure. 3) In one fusion reaction nearly $24.7MeV$ energy is released. 4) For the same mass, the energy released in fusion process is much more than that in the fission process.

6) Limited amount of fissionable substance is available in nature. 7) Fission process can be controlled. Nuclear reactor is based on the controlled fission reaction. 8) Nuclear bomb is based on the uncontrolled fission reaction.	5) The fissionable substance is not radioactive, so it does not give out any harmful radiations and disposal of its waste is also not difficult. 6) The fissionable substance is found in abundance. 7) Fusion reaction cannot be controlled. This is why fusion reactor could not be constructed so far. 8) Hydrogen bomb is based on the uncontrolled fusion reaction.

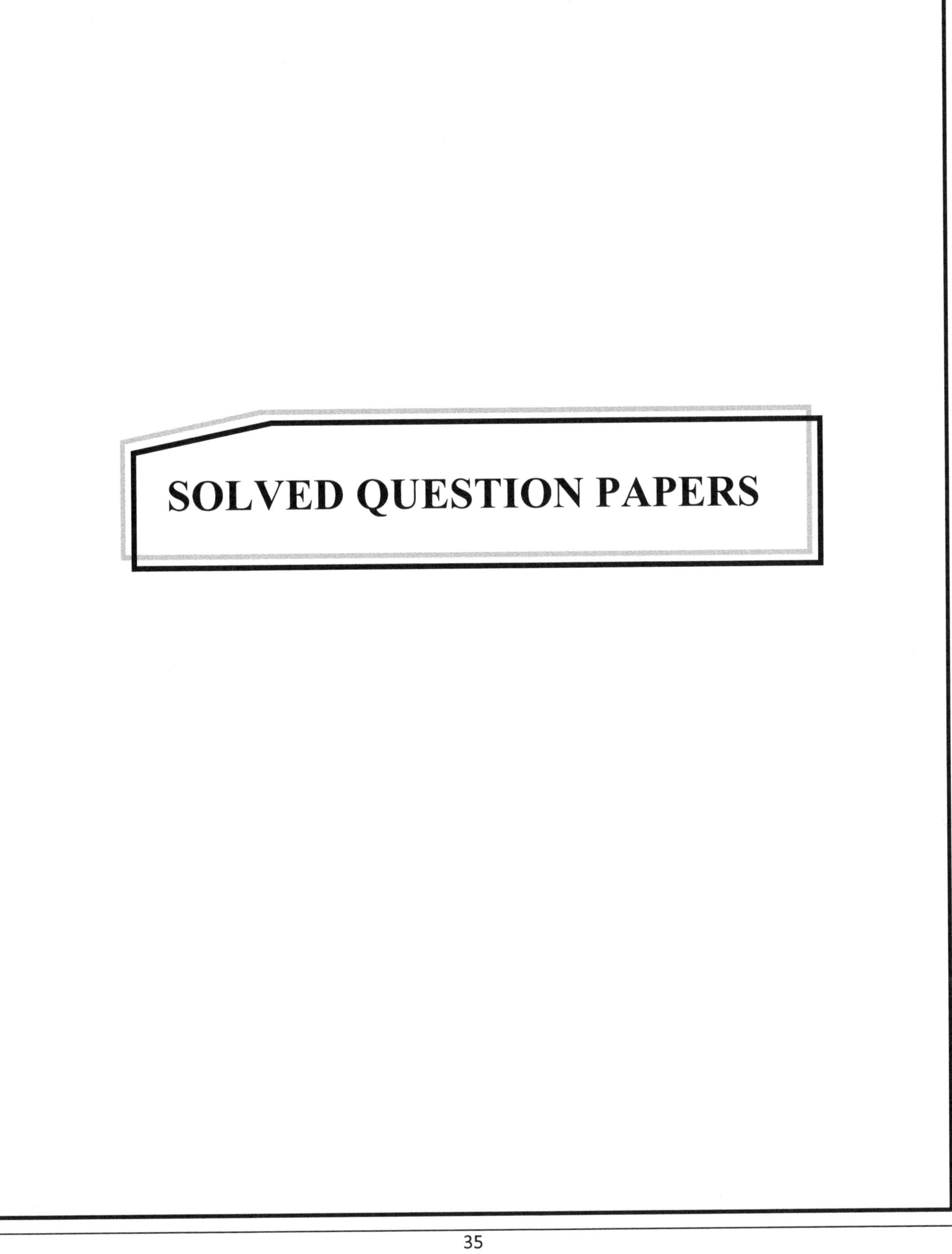

SOLVED QUESTION PAPERS

ICSE SEMESTER 2 EXAMINATION
MODEL PAPER-01 PHYSICS
(SCIENCE PAPER 1)

Maximum Marks: 40
Time allowed: One and a half hours

Attempt all questions from **Section A** and any three questions from **Section B.**
The intended marks for questions or parts of questions are given in brackets [].

(SECTION A [10 marks]
(Attempt all questions.)

Question 1:

Choose the correct answers to the questions from the given options. (Do not copy the question, Write the correct answer only.)

(i) Which of the following actions will increase the frequency of the note played on a guitar string?
(a) increasing the mass of the string
(b) decreasing the tension in the string
(c) fingering the string
(d) plucking the string harder

Solution: correct option is (c)

(ii) Rheostat is connected with circuit in connection.
(a) Series
(b) Parallel
(c) Either series or parallel
(d) None of these

Solution: correct option is (a)

(iii) Which of the following has maximum current?
(a) 100W-220V
(b) 10W-220V
(c) 200W-200V
(d) 500W-250V

Solution: correct option is (d)

(iv)What properties does a loud, shrill whistle have?

(a) high amplitude, high frequency
(b) high amplitude, low frequency
(c) low amplitude, high frequency
(d) low amplitude, low frequency

Solution: correct option is (a)

(v) As per Ohm's law, if the resistance of a conductor is doubled, what will be the effect on the current flowing through it?
a) it gets doubled
(b) it gets halved
(c) it increases 4 times
(d) No change

Solution: correct option is (b)

(vi) Which is the direction of magnetic field inside a magnet?
(a) from south pole to north pole
(b) from north pole to south pole
(c) from north pole till centre of the magnet
(d) None of the above

Solution: correct option is (a)

ii) Which of the following gives us the mass number of an atom?
(a) total number of electrons
(b) total number of neutrons
(c) total number of nucleons
(d) None of the above

Solution: correct option is (c)

(viii) The purpose of a rheostat is:
a) Increase the magnitude of current only
(b) Decrease the magnitude of current only
(c) Increase or decrease the magnitude of current
(d) None of these

Solution: correct option is (c)
(ix) When a 40V battery is connected across an unknown resistor there is a current of 100 mA in the circuit. Find the value of the resistance of the resister:
(a) 5000 Ω
(b) 800 Ω
(c) 0.8 Ω
(d) none of these

Solution: correct option is (d)

(x) An immersion heater of 396 W, changes 60g of ice at -12^0C into water at 40^0C. If the specific heat capacity of ice is $2Jg^{-1}C^{-1}$, calculate the specific latent heat of fusion of ice, when the heater is switched on for 1 min and 20 s.

(a) 345J/g
(b) 3360J/g
(c) 336J/g
(d) 236J/g

Solution: correct option is (c)

[Hint: use equation]

$MC_{ice} \times \Delta t + ML_{ice} + MC_{water} \Delta t = \text{Power} \times \text{time}$

SECTION B [30 marks]

(Attempt any three questions from this Section.)

Question 2

i. An electric bulb is rated 250W - 230V. What information does this convey? **[3]**

ii. 10,125J of heat energy boils off 4.5 g of water at 100°C to steam at 100°C. Find the specific latent heat of steam. **[3]**

iii. A stringed musical instrument, such as the Sitar, is provided with a number of wires of different thicknesses. Explain the reason for this. **[4]**

Solution:

(i)P =250 w
V = 230 v

Rating of Bulb it means if we connect the terminal of bulb with supply of 230 v it will produce 250 joule energy in 1 s.

(ii) Q = 10125 J
m = 4.5g

100° C water $\xrightarrow{Q = mL}$ 100°C steam

Q = mL
10125 = 4.5 L

$\text{Steam} = \frac{10125}{4.5} = \frac{2250\ J}{g}$

(iii)Wire of different thickness is provided with sitar, guitar etc. for producing sound of different frequency.

Question 3

(1)The following diagram shows a coil X connected to a sensitive Centre-zero galvanometer G and a coil P connected to a d.c. supply through a switch S. Describe the observation when the switch S is **[4]**

(i) closed suddenly,
(ii) then kept closed,

(iii) finally opened. Name and state the law which explains the above observations.

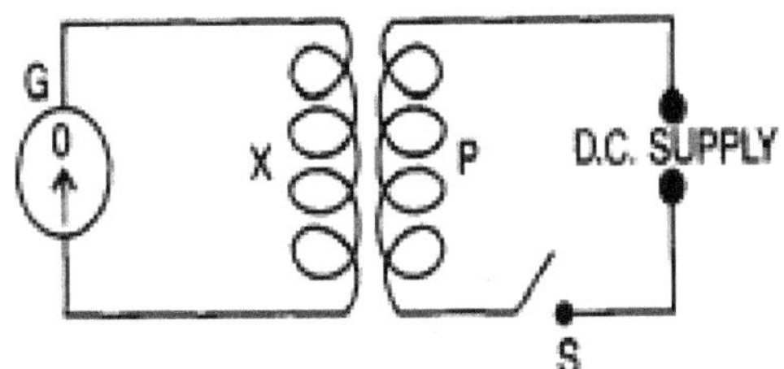

(a)An atomic nucleus denoted by $_{Z}X^{A}$ emits an alpha particle. Write an equation to show the formation of the daughter product. [3]

(b) Two wires of the same material and same length have radii r_1 and r_2 respectively. Compare (i) their resistances, (ii) resistivities [4]

Solution:

(i) When switch 's' closed suddenly there is deflection in galvanometer due induced current in coil 'x'.

(ii) No deflection in (G) because induced current is not produced due to no change in magnetic flux.

(iii) When key is open there is change in magnetic flux is which induced current is produced hence (G) show deflection in opposite direction.

Solution:

(iii) **a** $_{z}X^{A} - \alpha \rightarrow {}_{z-2}Y^{A-4} + {}_{2}He^{4} + E$ **α- particle.**

b(i) Let the length of wire l

Area of wire $A_1 = \pi r_1^2$

$A_2 = \pi r_2^2$

Let their Resistance one R_1 and R_2

$$\frac{R_1}{R_2} = \frac{l_1}{l_2} \times \frac{A_2}{A_1} = \frac{l}{l} \times \frac{\pi r_2^2}{\pi r_1^2}$$

$$R_1 : R_2 = r_2^2 : r_1^2$$

Material is same

Their resistivity will be same

$$\rho_1 : \rho_2 = 1:1$$

Question 4

(i) Two waves of the same pitch have their amplitudes in the ratio 1: 3. What will be the ratio of their Loudness?

(ii) A piece of ice is heated at a constant rate. The variation of temperature with heat input is shown in a graph below:

(a) What are represented by AB and CD?

(b) What conclusion can you draw regarding DE region of the graph?

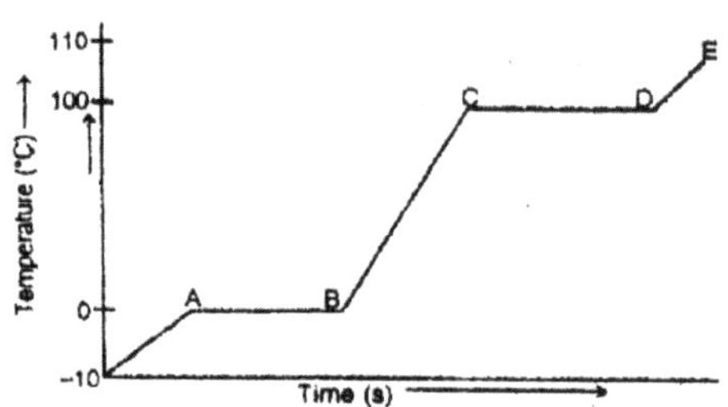

(iv)4 tube lights of 40 W each and 2 fans of 100 W each are connected to 200 V mains and operate on the average 8 hours a day. If energy costs Rs. 1.50 per kWh, calculate monthly bill.

Solution:

(i) Loudness $\propto$ (amplitude)^2

Loudness ratio = 1:9

(ii) (a) AB $\Rightarrow$ shows change of state (ice converted into water i.e., melting).

CD $\Rightarrow$ shows change of state (water converted into steam i.e., boiling)

(b) In DE region temperature of steam increases.

(iii)

4 Tube lights

40 w- 200 V

t = 8 h/ day

$W_1 = \frac{p \times t}{1000}$

$W_1 = \frac{40 \times 8}{1000} \times 4$

W_1 = 1.28kwh / day

2 fans

100 w – 200 V

t = 8h /day

$W_2 = \frac{p \times t}{1000}$

$W_2 = \frac{100 \times 8}{1000} \times 2$

$\frac{100 \times 8 \times 2}{1000}$

$W_2 = \frac{1.6 \text{kwh}}{\text{day}}$

Total energy consumed per day = 2.88 kWh

in one month = 30 × 2.88

= 86.40kwh

monthly bill = 86.4 × 1.5

= 129.60

Question 5

(i) $^{27}_{12}Mg \xrightarrow{\beta} Al \xrightarrow{\gamma}$

In the above nuclear reaction. (a) $_{12}Mg^{27}$ emits β, γ-particle and is transformed to aluminum. What is the mass number and the atomic number of aluminums? (b) Aluminum emits γ ray. What is the resulting nucleus?

(ii) In the dig. shown the cell and the ammeter both have negligible resistance. The resistors are identical. With the switch K open, the ammeter reads 0.6A. What will be the ammeter reading when the switch is closed?

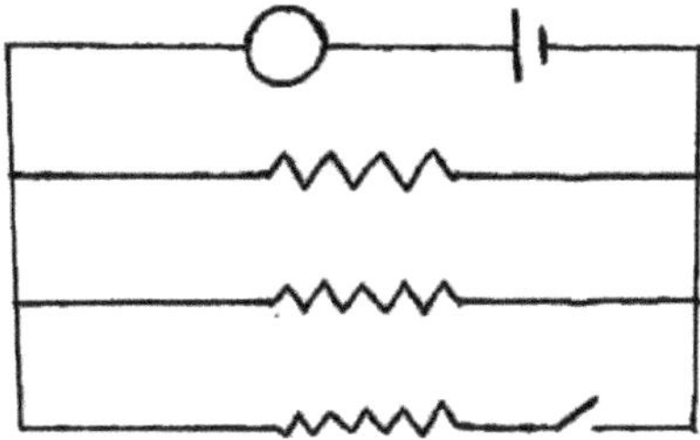

(iii) A refrigerator converts 100 g of water at 20°C to ice at -10°C in 73.5 min. Calculate the average rate of heat extraction in watt. The specific heat capacity of water is 4.2 J $g^{-1}\ {}^0C^{-1}$ and specific latent heat of ice is 336 J /g. The specific heat capacity of ice is 2.1 J $g^{-1}\ {}^0C^{-1}$.

Solution:

(I)(a)

$$^{27}Mg \xrightarrow{-\beta} {}^{27}_{13}Al \xrightarrow{-\gamma} {}^{27}_{13}Al^* + \Delta E$$

mass no of $Al =$ 27 [* Energy level]

Atomic no of $Al = 13$

(b) when Aluminum emits y-Ray there in no change in atomic no and mass no but energy level will change.

(ii)

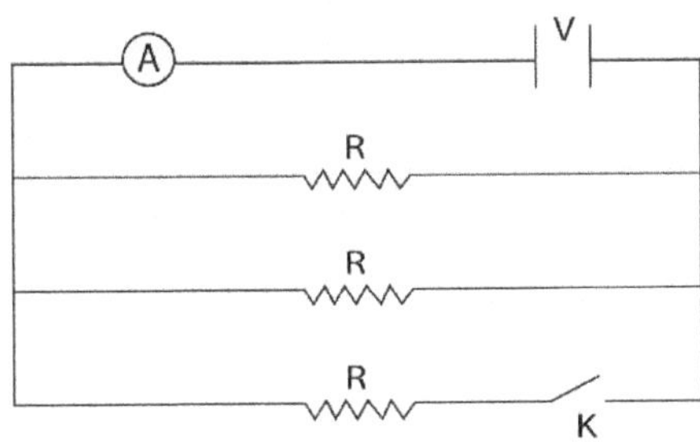

when k is open

Total Resistance in circuit

$$\frac{1}{R}+\frac{1}{R} = \frac{1}{R_{\text{Tatal}}}$$

$$R_{\text{Total}} = \frac{R}{2}$$

$$\therefore \text{ by ohm's Law: } i = \frac{V}{R}$$

$$0.6 = \frac{V}{\frac{R}{2}} = \frac{2V}{R}$$

$$V = \frac{0.6R}{2}$$

when switch is closed

$$\frac{1}{R_{\text{Total}}} = \frac{1}{R}+\frac{1}{R}+\frac{1}{R} = \frac{3}{R}$$

$$R_{\text{Total}} = \frac{R}{3}$$

$$R_{\text{Total}} = \frac{R}{3}$$

$$\therefore\ i = \frac{V}{R_{\text{Total}}} = \frac{\frac{0.6R}{2}}{R/3}$$

$$\boxed{i = 0.9A}$$

(iii)

(iii) 100g water at $20°C$ ⟶ ice at

→ $10°C$

$20°C$ water mc $\Delta\theta$

0^0 C $_{\text{ice}}$ $\xrightarrow{\text{m } L_{ice}}$ 0^0 C of ice

0^0C_{water} $\xrightarrow{\text{m } C_{ice}\, \Delta\theta}$ - 10^0 C of ice

Total heat released = m C $_{\text{water}}$ $\Delta\theta$

$100 \times 4.2 \times 20 + 100 \times 336 + 100 \times 10 \times 21$

$= 8400 + 33600 + 2100 = 44100J$

For Refrigerator Energy = Power × time

∴ by Principle of Calorimetry

P x 73.5 x 60 = 44100

$\boxed{\text{P = 10 w}}$

ICSE SEMESTER 2 EXAMINATION
MODEL PAPER-02 PHYSICS
(SCIENCE PAPER 1)

Maximum Marks: 40

Time allowed: One and a half hours

Attempt all questions from **Section A** and any three questions from **Section B.**
The intended marks for questions or parts of questions are given in brackets [ ].

SECTION A [10 marks]
(Attempt all questions.)

Question 1

Choose the correct answers to the questions from the given options. (Do not copy the question, Write the correct answer only.)

(i) The vibrations of a body in presence of an externa periodic force is called as,

(A) Free vibration

(B) Resonance

(C) Forced vibration

(D) Damped vibration

Solution: correct option is (c)

(ii) m gram hot water at t°C is all added to 3m gram of cold water at 10°C. If the final temperature of the mixture is 20°C, then the value of t is:

(A) 30°C (B) 40°C

(C) 50°C (D) 60°C

Solution:

(ii)

Hot water	Cold water
$m_1 = m$ gram	$m_2 = 3m$ gram
$t_1 = t°C$	$t_2 = 10°C$
$SHC = C$	$SHC = C$

Final temp20^{0}c

By Principle of calorimetry

$$m_1c_1\Delta t_1 = m_2c_2\Delta t_2$$
$$mc(t-20) = 3mc(20-10)$$
$$t-20 = 30$$
$$\boxed{t = 50°C \quad \text{option } C}$$

(iii) Household electrical appliances are connected in
(A) Series
(B) Parallel
(C) Either series or parallel
(D) Both in series in parallel

Solution: correct option is (B)

(iv) Hans Oersted in his experiments observed that
(A) When a current is passed through a conducting wire a magnetic field is produced in it.
(B) When a conducting wire is placed in a magnetic field an e.m.f. is induced across its two ends.
(C) When direction of the current passing through a conducting wire is reversed the deflection of a magnetic needle placed closed to it is also reversed.
(D) Both (A) and (B)

Solution: correct option (D)

(v) . Amount of heat energy required to melt 5 kg of ice at 0°C is
(Specific latent heat of ice = 336 J /g)
(A) 1680000J
(B) 1680J
(C) 168×10^3J
(D)3360J

Solution: correct option is (d)

(vi) Which of the following is a non-Ohmic conductor?
(A) Filament of a bulb
(B) Nichrome
(C) Copper
(D) Silicon

Solution: correct option is (D)

(vii) 1 calorie is correctly defined as
(A) Heat energy required to raise the temperature 1g of water from 14.5° C to 15.5°C.
(B) Heat energy required to raise the temperature 1g of water by 1°C.
(C) Heat energy required to raise the temperature 1g of water 4°C to 5°C.
(D) Heat energy required to raise the temperature 1g of water 0°C to 1°C.

Solution: correct option is (A)

(viii) Which of the flowing statements is correct?

(A) Strength of the magnetic field produced by an electromagnet cannot be easily changed.
(B) Polarity of an electromagnet cannot be reversed.
(C) It produces the magnetic field as long as the current flows in the coil.
(D) It cannot be easily demagnetized

Solution: correct option is (C)

(ix) Quality of a musical sound depends on the
(A) Pitch
(B) Waveform
(C) Loudness
(D) none
Solution: correct option is (B)

(x), When a cell is in use
(A) Its terminal voltage is equal to the electromotive force
(B) Its terminal voltage is greater than the electromotive force
(C) Its terminal voltage is less than the electromotive force
(D) The relation between its terminal voltage and electromotive force depends on its internal resistance

Solution: correct option is (C)

SECTION B [30 marks]

(Attempt any three questions from this Section.)

Question 2 [3]
(i) (a) Define calorimetry.
(b) Name the material used for making a calorimetry
(c) Why is a Calorimeter made up of thin sheets of the above material answered in (b)?

(ii) (a) Shruti draws magnetic field lines close to the axis of a current carrying circular loop. As she moves away from the centre of circular loop, she observes that the lines keep on diverging. Explain the reason for her observation. [3]
(b) Write two properties of magnetic field lines

(iii) (a) what is an ohmic resistor? [4]
(b) Two copper wires are of the same length, but one is thicker than the other
(i)Which wire will have more resistance?
(ii) Which wire will have more specific resistance

Solution:
(i) (a) it in the branch of Physics in which we deal with measurement of heat lost or gained by substance.
(b) Copper
(c) Calorimeter is made of thin copper sheet so that its heat Capacity becomes small.
(ii) (a)Inside the solenoid magnetic fields are parallel, it diverges 'so that they can make close loop and avoid intersection.

(b) 1) They never intersect each other.

2) If we draw a tangent at any point of on magnetic field lines it represents the direction of magnetic field at that point.

(iii) (a) conductor which obeys ohms law V/I=R is Called ohmic conductor. i.e., silver.

(b) (i) Thinner wire has move Resistance $\left(R \propto \frac{1}{A}\right)$

(ii) Both have same specific Resistance.

Question 3

(i) The total resistance of two resistors when connected in series is 9 Ω and when connected in parallel, their total resistance becomes 2Ω. Find the value of each resistance. [3]

(ii) Radioactive nuclei can decay in two different ways, each of these brings about a change in the mass number A and the proton number Z of the decaying parent nucleus. Write appropriate equation to show the effect of each type of decay on both A and Z. [3]

(iii) Water falls from a height of 20 m at a rate of 100 kg/ s. How many calories of heat will be produced per second on striking with the earth? Assume that the whole energy is converted into heat. [4]

Solution:

(i) $R_1 + R_2 = 9 - (1)$

$$\frac{1}{R_1} + \frac{1}{R_2} = \frac{1}{2}$$
$$\frac{R_2 + R_1}{R_1 R_2} = \frac{1}{2}$$
$$R_1 R_2 = 18$$
$$R_1(9 - R_1) = 18$$
$$R_1^2 - 9R_1 + 18 = 0$$

on solving quadratic equation

$$R_1 = 3\Omega, 6\Omega$$
$$\therefore R_2 = 6\Omega, 3\Omega$$

Ans: 3Ω and 6Ω

(ii) Radioactive nuclei decayed in two different ways.

1 Alpha decay

$$zX^A - \alpha \longrightarrow {}^{A-4}_{z-2}Y + 2H^4 + \Delta E$$

2 Beta decay

$$_2X^A - \beta \longrightarrow {}_{z+1}^{A}Y + \beta^0 + \Delta E$$

(iii) Potential energy of water converted into heat energy $\therefore\ mgh = Q$ (heat per second)

Q = 100.0 x 9.8 x 20 J/s

Q = 19600 J/s

Heat energy produced in calorie

$Q = \frac{19600}{4.2} = 4666.6$ cal.

Question 4

(i) . Arrange α, β and γ rays in ascending order with respect to them [4]

a. Penetrating power.

b. lionising power.

c. biological effect

(ii) When a tuning fork, struck by a rubber pad is held over a length of air column in a tube, it produces a loud sound for a fixed length of the air column. [3]

(a) Name the above phenomenon.

(b) How does the frequency of the loud sound compare with that of the tuning fork?

(c) State the unit for measuring loudness.

(iii) A body of mass "m_1" of a substance of specific heat capacity "c_1", at a temperature t_1 is mixed with another body of mass "m_2" of specific heat capacity "c_2" at a lower temperature t_2. Deduce an expression for the temperature of the mixture t_3. [4]

Solution: -(i) a) Penetrating power $\Rightarrow \alpha, \beta, \gamma$

b) Ionizing power $\Rightarrow \gamma, \beta, \alpha$

c) Biological effect = α, β, γ

(ii) (a) Resonance of sound wave.

(b) Frequency of loud sound is equal to or integral multiple of frequency of tuning fork.

(c) decibel

(iii)

Hot body	Cold Body
mas = m_1	mass = m_2
SHC = C_1	SHC = C_2
Temp. = t_1	Temp = t_2

Final temp = t_3

By Principle of Calorimetry $m_1c_1(t_1 - t_3) = m_2c_2(t_3 - t_2)$

$$m_1c_1(t_1 - t_3) = m_2c_2(t_3 - t_2)$$
$$m_1c_1t_1 - m_1c_1t_3 = m_2c_2t_3 - m_2c_2t$$
$$m_1c_1t_1 - m_2c_1t_3 = m_2c_2t_3 - m_2c_2t_2$$
$$m_1c_1t_1 + m_2c_2t_2 = t_3(m_2c_2 + m_1c_1)$$

Question 5

(i) Calculate the conductivity of a wire of length 2 m, area of cross section 2 cm^2 and resistance is 10^{-4} Ω. [4]

(ii) A piece of iron of mass 2.0 kg has a thermal capacity of 966 J/°C. [3]

(a) How much heat is needed to warm it by 15 °C?

(b) What is its specific heat capacity in SI Unit?

(iii) (a) Two sets A and B of three bulbs each, are glowing in two separate rooms. When one of the bulbs in set A is fused, the other two bulbs also cease to glow. But in set B, when one bulb fuses, the other two bulbs continue to glow. Explain why this phenomenon occurs?

(b) Why do we prefer arrangements of set B for house circuit?

[3]

Solution:

$$\text{(i) } (\sigma) \text{ Conductivity } = \frac{l}{RA}$$

$$A = 2 \times 10^{-4} m^2, l = 2m, R = 10^{-4}\Omega$$

$$\sigma = \frac{2}{10^{-4} \times 2 \times 10^{-4}}$$

$$\sigma = 1 \times 10^{8} \frac{sieman}{m}$$

(ii) (a) Heat needed $\boldsymbol{Q = c' \cdot \Delta t}$

$$\begin{aligned} Q &= c' \cdot \Delta t \\ &= 966 \times 15 J \\ &= 14490 J \end{aligned}$$

(ii) (b)

SI Unit = 483 J kg $^{-1}$ k^{-1}

(iii) (a) The bulbs of set A are Connected in series. Therefore, when one bull is fused, the current Stops flowing, whereas the bulbs of Set *B* one connected in parallel. When one bulb fuses, the current House through the other bulbs.

(b) We prefer set 'B' for house circuit because one defective appliance should not stop other appliance.

ICSE SEMESTER 2 EXAMINATION
MODEL PAPER-03 PHYSICS
(SCIENCE PAPER 1)

Maximum Marks: 40

Time allowed: One and a half hours

Attempt all questions from **Section A** and any three questions from **Section B.**
The intended marks for questions or parts of questions are given in brackets [ ].

(SECTION A [10 marks]
(Attempt all questions.)

Question 1

Choose the correct answers to the questions from the given options. (Do not copy the question, Write the correct answer only.)

(i) Conventionally, in a 3-pin plug, the — pin is for earthing, — pin is for live and — pin is for neutral.

(a) Top, right, left
(b) Top, left, right
(c) Right, top, left
(d) Left, top, right

Solution: correct option is (a)

(ii) Which one is an example for free vibration?

(a) A washing machine shakes due to an imbalance
(b) Pulling a string
(c) Pulling a child back on a swing and letting go
(d) none

Solution correct option is (d)

(iii) Ice _____ on melting. Wax___________ on melting.

(a) Expands, contracts.
(b) Contracts, expands.
(c) Expands, expands.
(d) Contracts, contracts.

Solution correct option is (b)

(iv) Magnitude of the force acting on a current carrying conductor placed in a magnetic field in a direction perpendicular to the field is

(a) Directly proportional to the time of flowing
(b) Directly proportional magnetic field
(c) Directly proportional temperature
(d) All of the above

Solution correct option is (b)

(v) The unit of electromotive force is:
(a) newton
(b) volt
(c) weber/ meter
(d) tesla

Solution correct option is (b)

(vi) Which of the following has highest specific heat capacity?
(a) oil
(b) sand
(c) water
(d) alcohol

Solution correct option is (c)

(vii) Pendulums A, B, C and D are tied to a flexible string PQ and are at rest. Pendulum C is disturbed. Which of the following statements is true?

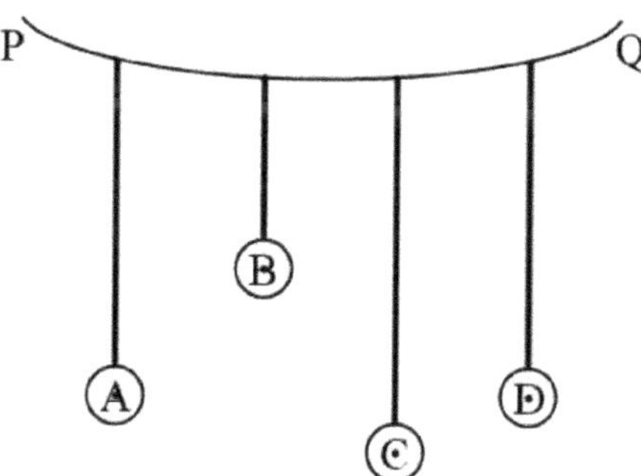

(a) Only pendulum C will start vibrating.
(b) Pendulums A, B, and D will also start vibrating but A and D will vibrate with the maximum amplitude.
(c) Pendulums A, B, and D will also start vibrating.
(d) Vibrations of pendulum C are forced vibrations.

Solution correct option is (b)

(viii) The diagram below shows a magnet moved near a coil along its axis. Which of the diagram shows correct flow of current during this motion?

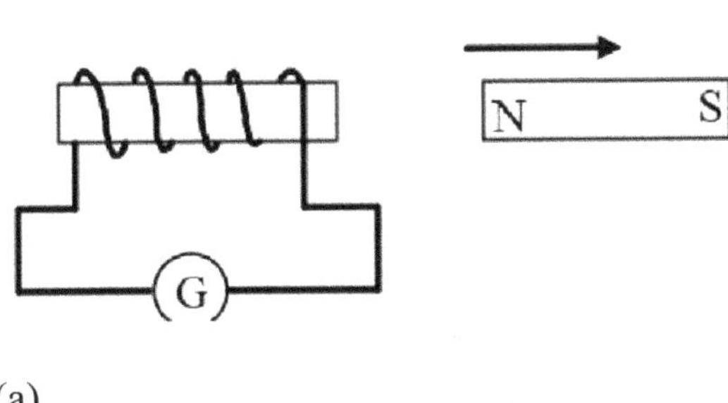

(a)

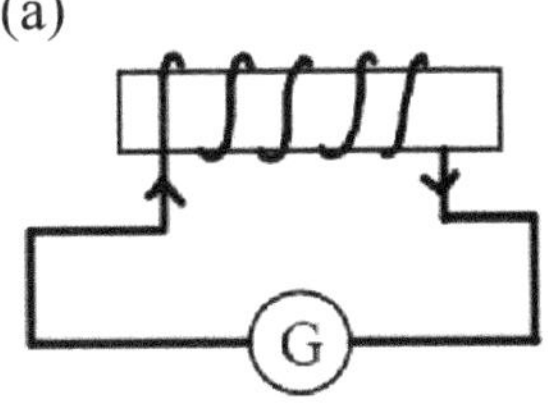

(b)

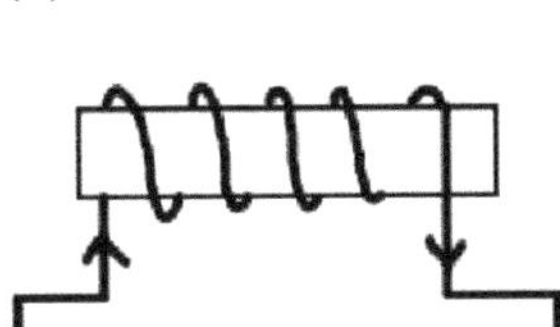

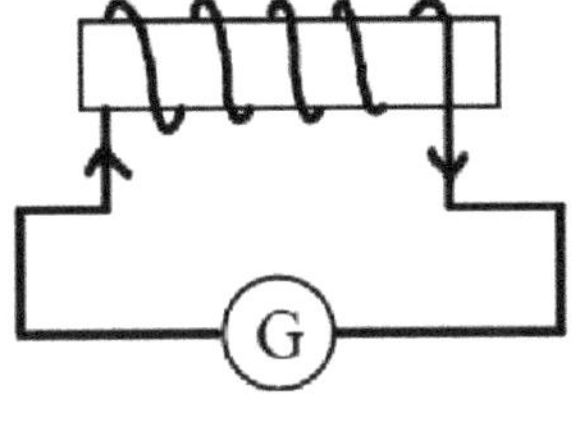

(c)

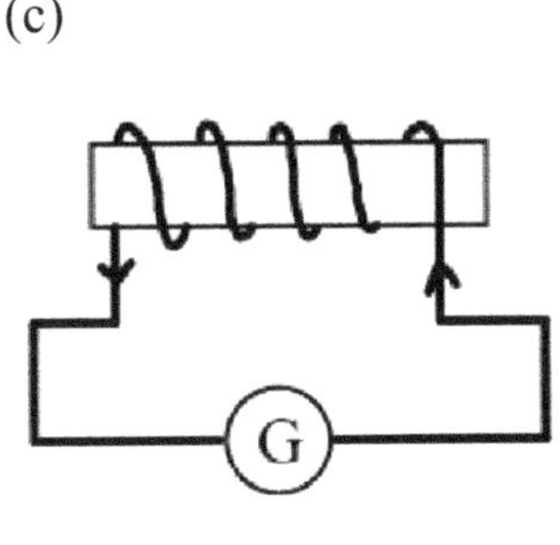

(d)

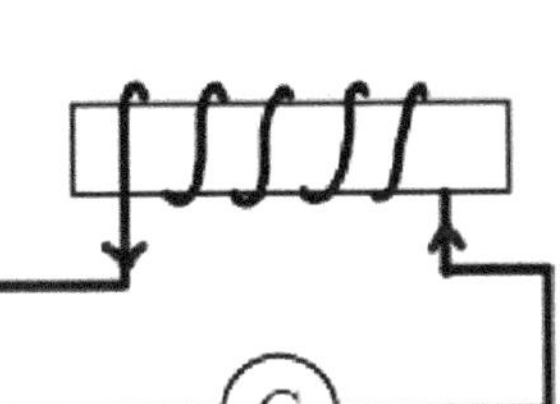

Solution correct option is (a)

(ix) The nuclear radiation which gets deflected towards negatively charged plate in an electric field **is:**
(a) Gamma
(b) Ultraviolet
(c) Beta
(d) Alpha

Solution correct option is (d)

(x) Resonance is:
(a) A forced vibration in which amplitude remains constant.
(b) A forced vibration in which frequency of forced vibration is greater than the free vibrations of the body.
(c) A forced vibration, in which frequency of forced vibration is equal to the free vibrations of the body.
(d) A forced vibration, in which frequency of forced vibration is less than the free vibrations of the body.

Solution correct option is (c)

SECTION B [30 marks]

(Attempt any three questions from this Section.)

Question 2

(i)
(a) Which will absorb more heat, 10 g of ice at 0^0C or 10 g of water at 0^0C? [3]
(b) For the same mass of ice and ice-cold water, why does ice produce more cooling than ice-cold water?

(ii) The diagram below shows a cooling curve for 200 g of water. The heat is extracted at the rate of 100 J/s. Answer the questions that follow: [3]

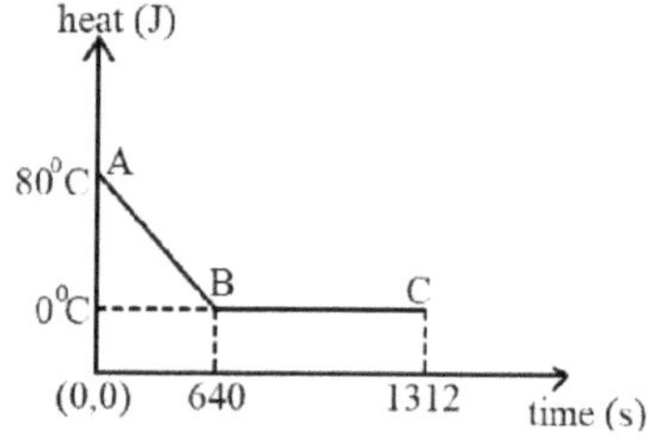

(a) Calculate specific heat capacity of water.
(b) Heat released in the region BC.

(iii) [4]
(a) Name the electrical appliance shown in the diagram below.
(b) Name the material of the wire used in this device.
(c) Name two important characteristics of this wire.

(i)

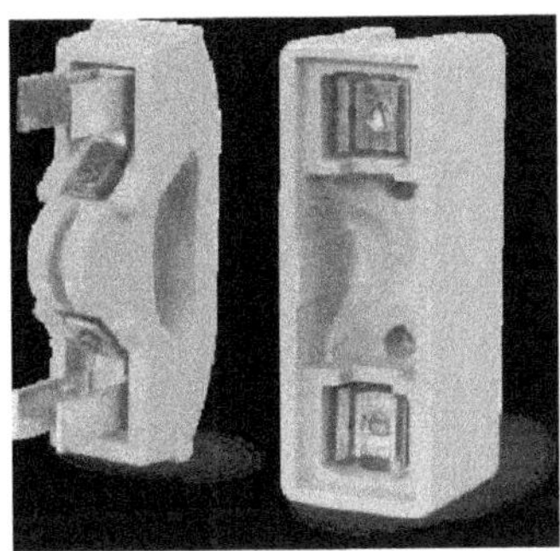

Solution

(i)(a) l0g ice at $0°c$ will absorb more energy as compared to $10g$ of water at $0°C$ because it takes latent heat for melting and becomes water at $0°C$.

(b)0^0C ice produces more cooling than water at $0°C$ because ice tote takeds talent heat from body that's why ice produce more cooling.

(ii) $(a)\ Q = mc\Delta\theta$

Heat extracted in 640 second

$$Q = P \times t = 100 \times 640J$$
$$\therefore\ 64000 = 200 \times C \times (80 - 0)$$
$$C = 4Jg^{-1}\,°C^{-1}$$

(b) Heat released in region $BC =$

$$Q \quad = p \times t = 100 \times 672$$
$$Q = 67200J$$

(iii) (a) Electric fuse

(b) alloy of tin and lead is used as fuse wire.

(c) (i) melting point of fuse wire should be low.

(ii) It should be good conductor of electricity.

Question 3

(i) [3]

(a) State the Faraday's laws of electromagnetic induction

(b) Name one electrical device which works on this principle.

(ii) [3]

(a) Which one of the following graphs A or B shows free vibrations in vacuum and which one shows free vibrations in a medium?

(b) How did you come to this conclusion.

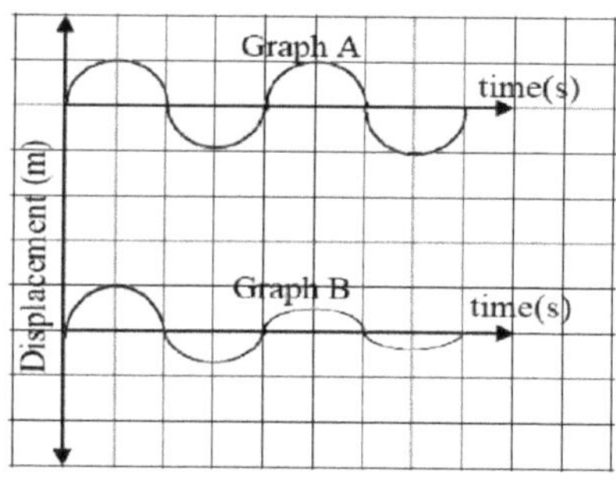

(iii) [4]

(a) Why is water used as a coolant in radiators of a car?
(b) Name the radioactive isotope used to find the age of fossils. Name the radioactive radiation which it emits

Solution:

(i) (a) whenever there is change in magnetic flux linked with coil, an induced emf is developed across the ends of coil. This phenomenon is known as electromagnetic induction. If circuit is closed an induced current is flowing through coil.
(b) Transformer.
(ii) Graph A free vibration.
(b) Amplitude of graph ' A ' is constants that shows it is free vibration.
(iii) (a) SHC of water is high and it takes we large amount of heat from body (thus we used water as coolant.
(b) $C-14$. Isotope is use to find the and of fossils. it emits Beta particle.

Question 4

(i)
Which contains more heat: 1 g sand at 100^0C or 1 g steam at 100^0C? Give reason. [4]

(ii) An electrical heater is rated 2A - 220 V. Find the monthly cost of using this heater for 30 hours if one kWh of electrical energy costs Rs 5.0. [3]

(iii)
Two metals A and B have specific heat capacities in the ratio 2:3. If they are supplied same amount of heat then [3]

(a) Which metal piece will show greater rise in temperature given their masses are the same?
(b) Which metal piece will have greater mass if the rise in temperature is the same for both metals?
(c) If the mass ratio of metal A and metal B is 3:5 then calculate the ratio in which their temperatures rise.
(d) If specific heat capacity of metal A is 0.26 $Jg^{-1}\,{}^0C^{-1}$ then calculate the specific heat capacity of metal B

Solution

(i) $1g$ steam has more heat because it contains latent heat while sand does not.
(ii) Electrical energy consumed by heater

$$w=\frac{vit}{1000}$$

$$w = \frac{220 \times 2 \times 30}{1000} = \frac{132}{10} = 13.2 \text{ kwh}$$

∴ Cost of electricity for one month

$$= 13.2 \times 5 = \text{Rs. } 66.0$$

(iii) SHC. Of A = 2x

SHC. Of B = 3x

(a) Metal A shows more rise in temperature because of low specific heat capacity.

(b) ∵ supplied energy is same

$$Q_A = Q_B$$

$$M_A \cdot 2x\Delta\theta = m_B 3x\Delta\theta$$

$$\frac{m_A}{m_B} = \frac{3}{2} \quad M_A : m_B = 3:2$$

∴ metal A ' has more mass.

(c) mass Ratio $M_A : M_B = 3:5$

$$M_A = 3y, \ M_B = 5y$$

$$Q_A = Q_B$$

$$\therefore M_A 2x \times \Delta\theta_A = M_B \times 3x \times \Delta\theta_B$$

$$3y \times 2 \cdot \Delta\theta_A = 5y \times 3 \times \Delta\theta_B.$$

$$6\Delta\theta_A = 15\Delta\theta_B$$

$$\frac{\Delta\theta_A}{\Delta\theta_B} = \frac{15}{6}$$

Ratio of temp. = $\Delta\theta_A : \Delta\theta_B = 5:2$

(d) Ratio of SHC of A and $B = 2:3$

SHC of $A = 2x$

SHC of B = 3x

$2x = 0.26 J g^{-1}$

$2x = 0.26 J g^{-1}$

$x = 0.13 J g^{-1} \, {}^\circ C^{-1}$

∴ SHB of $B = 3x$

$= 3 \times 0.13 J \, g^{-1} \, {}^0C^{-1}$

SHC of $'B' = 0.39 J g^{-1} \, {}^\circ C'^{-1}$

Question 5

(i) [4]

Calculate the resistivity of a wire of length 2 m, area of cross section 2 cm^2 and resistance is 10Ω.

(ii) [3]

(a) Observe the diagram given below and state whether the bulb will glow or not when we switch on K.

(b) Is it safe to handle the bulb when the switch is OFF?

(c) Give a reason for your answer in (b).

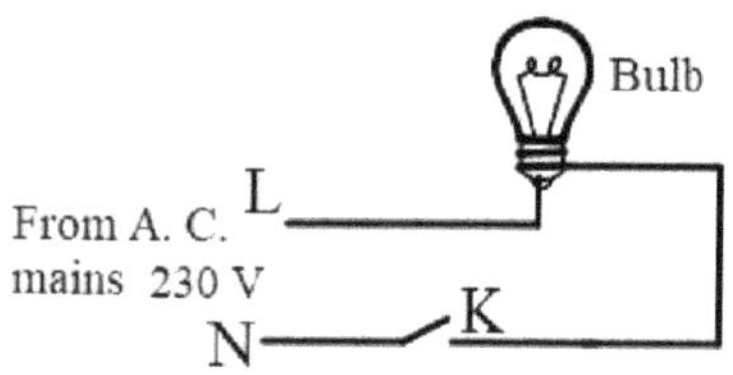

[3]

(iii)A nucleus $_{82}X^{194}$ emits an alpha particle

(a) What will be the atomic number of the daughter nucleus Y?

(b) What will be the number of neutrons in the daughter nucleus Y?

(c) Write a nuclear reaction showing the emission of this particle.

Solution: (1) $\rho = \frac{RA}{l}$

$l = 2m, R = 10\Omega, A = 2 \times 10^{-4}m^2$

$$\rho = \frac{10 \times 2 \times 10^{-4}}{2} = 1 \times 10^{-3}\Omega - m$$

Resistivity $= 1 \times 10^{-3}\Omega - m$

(ii) (a) Yes bulb will glow.

(b) No, because current will reach to bulb.

(C) For safety switch is always connected in line wire before the device.

(iii) (a) $^{194}_{82}X - \alpha \longrightarrow_{80} Y^{190} + 2He^4 + 4E$ Atomic number = 80

(b) No of neutron in daughter nueleus y = 190 – 80 = 110

(c) $_{82}X^{194} - \underset{\text{Alpha}}{\alpha \longrightarrow} {}^{190}_{80}Y + \underset{\text{Alpha}}{2He^4} + \Delta E$

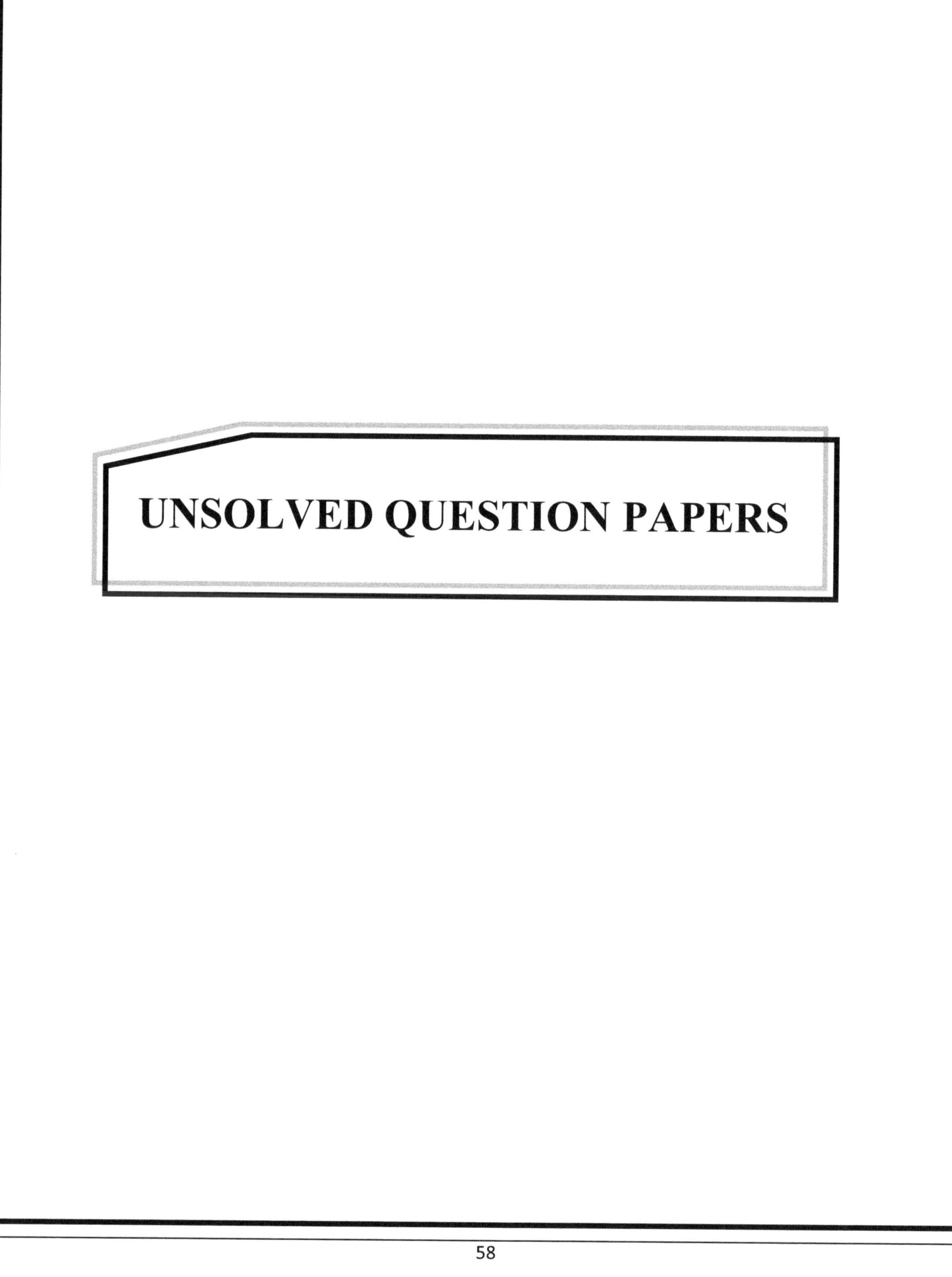

UNSOLVED QUESTION PAPERS

ICSE SEMESTER 2 EXAMINATION
MODEL PAPER 01 PHYSICS
(SCIENCE PAPER 1)
Maximum Marks: 40
Time allowed: One and a half hours

Attempt all questions from **Section A** and any three questions from **Section B.**

SECTION A [10 Marks]

(Attempt all questions.)

Question 1

Choose the correct answers to the questions from the given options. (Do not copy the question, Write the correct answer only.)

(i) The rate of flow of electric charge is known as :
(a) Electric potential
(b) Electric conductance
(c) Electric current
(d) Electrical Conductor

(ii) Expansion in a substance is:
(a) Directly proportional to rise in the temperature
(b) Inversely proportional to rise in the temperature
(c) Independent of rise temperature
(d) Cannot say

(iii) On reversing the direction of current in a wire, the magnetic field produced by it:
(a)Gets reversed in direction
(b)Increases in strength
(c)Decreases in strength
(d)Remains unchanged in strength and direction

(iv) Find the equivalent resistance between A and B of Fig.

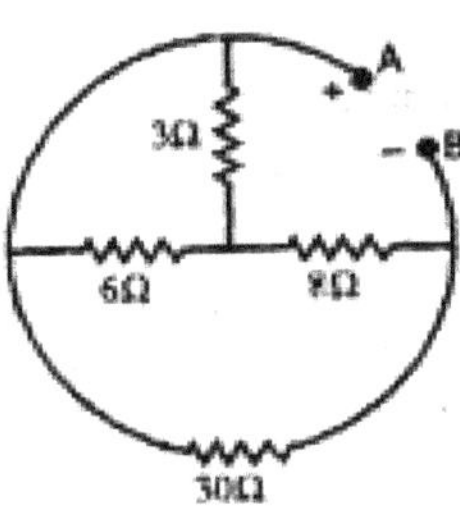

(a)5.5 Ω

(b)1.5 Ω

(c)7.5 Ω

(d)8.5 Ω

(v) How much heat would be required to convert 14kg of ice at 0°C into water of 0°C?
(a) 4704 J
(b) 4704 kJ
(c) 336 J
(d) 336 kJ

(vi) A step-up transform has a turns ratio of 1: 200. An alternating supply of 15 V is connected across the primary coil. The secondary voltage should be:
(a)3000 volts
(b)1500 volts
(c)1000 volts
(d)2000 volts

(vii) Which of the following frequencies is audible to human beings?
(a)5 Hz
(b) 20 kHz
(c) 5 kHz
(d) 50 kHz

(viii) Two bulbs A and B are connected in series with a cell. Resistance of the bulb A is Ra and resistance of the bulb B is Rb. The ratio of the currents in the bulb A to the bulb B is
(a)$R_a : R_b$
(b)1: 1
(c)$R_b : R_a$
(d)Data insufficient

(viii) Fleming's right-hand rule is used to find the direction of
(a)Magnetic field
(b) Electric field
(c) Induced current
(d) Mechanical force

(ix) In air, alpha particles have range of
(a)few centimetres
(b)several thousand meters
(c)several hundred meters
(d)several meters

SECTION - II [30 marks]

(Attempt any three questions from this section)

2. (i) In the diagram given below, A, B and C are three ammeters. The ammeter B reads 0.5 A. All the ammeters have negligible resistance. Calculate- [3]
(a) the readings of the ammeters A and C,

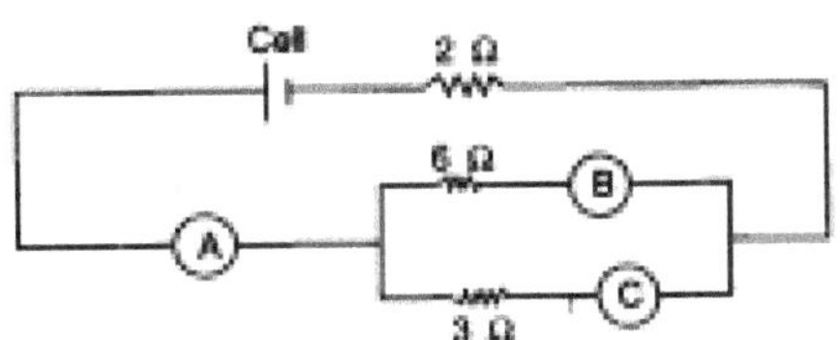

(b) the total resistance of the circuit, and

(c) the e.m.f. of the cell.

(ii) (a) Draw a neat, labelled diagram of an a.c. generator.

(b) What is the magnitude of the emf induced in the coil when its plane becomes parallel to the magnetic held? [3]

(iii). A vessel of negligible heat capacity contains 40 g of ice in it at 0°C. 8 g of steam at 100°C is passedinto the ice to melt it. Find the final temperature of the contents of the vessel. (Specific latent heat ofvaporization of steam, = 2268 J/g; Specific latent heat of fusion of ice = 336 J/g and Specific heat capacityof water = 4.2 J/g°C) [4]

3. (i) A copper colorimeter of mass 50 g contains 100 g of water at 20 ^{0}C. A metallic piece of mass 250 g isheated to 100 ^{0}C and is then dropped into the calorimeter. The contents of the calorimeter are wellstirred and its final highest temperature is recorded to be 28 ^{0}C. If the specific heat capacity of water is 4.2 $J^{-1} g^{-1} {}^0C^{-1}$ and of copper is 0.4 $J^{-1} g^{-1} {}^0C^{-1}$, find: [3]

(i) the heat gained by water (ii) the heat gained bycalorimeter (iii) total heat supplied by the metal piece, and (iv) the specific heat capacity of metal. [3]

(ii). (a) What is the principle on which sonar is based?

(a) Calculate the minimum distance at which a person should stand in front of a reflecting surface so that can hear a distinct echo. (Take speed of sound in air = 350 m s^{-1}.)

(iii) (a) Draw a simple labelled diagram of a free Vibration and damped vibration. [4]

(b) What is the function of the split rings in a d.c. motor?

(c) State one advantage of a.c. over d.c.

4. (i) A bulb is connected to a battery of p.d. 4 V and internal resistance 2.5 Ω. A steady current of 0.5 A flowsthrough the circuit. Calculate (a) the total energy supplied by the battery in 10 minutes, (b) the resistance of the bulb, and (c) the energy dissipated in the bulb in 10 minutes. [4]

(iii) 200 g of a solid at 100°C is dropped into a copper calorimeter of mass 100 g containing water weighing150 g at 40°C. The final temperature reached is 50° C. Calculate the specific heat capacity of solid. Given that the specific heat capacity of copper is 0.4 J $kg^{-1} {}^0C^{-1}$ and of water is 4.2 J $kg^{-1} {}^0C^{-1}$.

(iii). (a) An atomic nucleus A is composed of 84 protons and 128 neutrons. The nucleus A emits an α-particle and is transformed into a nucleus B. What is the composition of B? [3]

(b) The nucleus B emits β -panicle and is transformed into a nucleus C. What is the composition of C?

(c) What is the mass number of the nucleus A?

(d) Does the composition of nucleus C change if it emits a ϒ-radiation?

5. (i) A battery of e.m.f. 20 V and internal resistance 2 Ω is connected to two resistors of 3ohm and 6 ohms joined [4]

(a) in series, (b) in parallel. Find in each case the electrical energy spent per minute in 3-ohm resistor.

(ii) Differentiate between forced vibration and resonance. [3]

(iii). In a laboratory experiment for finding specific latent heat of ice, 100 g of water at 30°C was taken ina calorimeter made of copper and of mass 10g. When 10 g of ice at 0°C was added to the mixture and kept within the liquid till the ice melted completely, the final temperature of the mixture was found to be 20°C. [3]

(a) What is the total quantity of water in the calorimeter at 20° C?

(b) Specific heat capacities of water and copper being 4.2 J $g^{-1}\,{}^{0}C^{-1}$ and 0.4 J $g^{-1}\,{}^{0}C^{-1}$ respectively, what quantity of heat would each release in cooling down to 20°C from the initial stage?

(c) Write an expression for the heat gained by ice on melting.

(d) Calculate the value of the latent heat of fusion of ice from the data discussed above.

ICSE SEMESTER 2 EXAMINATION
MODEL PAPER 02 PHYSICS
(SCIENCE PAPER 2)

Maximum Marks: 40
Time allowed: One and a half hours

Attempt all questions from Section A and any three questions from Section B.

SECTION A (Attempt all questions.)

Question 1

Choose the correct answers to the questions from the given options. (Do not copy the question, Write the correct answer only.)

(i)Material is used to prepare the filament of a bulb.
(a)Tungsten
(b)Lead
(c)Copper
(d)Platinum

(ii)In the earth's magnetic field alone, The compass needle rest along in which direction?
(a)East – west
(b) North east
(c) South – North
(d) No Fixed direction

(iii)The wavelength of an ultrasonic wave is:
(a)the same as that of the audible sound
(b) very low
(c) more than that of audible sound
(d) very high

(iv)2000 J of energy is needed to heat 1kg of paraffin through 1°C. How much energy is needed to heat 10kg of paraffin through 2°C?
(a) 4000 J
(b) 10,000 J
(c) 20,000 J
(d) 40,000 J

(v)A process in which heavy nucleus splits into two by bombarding a slow-moving neutron is called
(a)Radioactivity
(b)Nuclear fusion
(c)Nuclear fission
(d)Nuclear splitting

(vi) Which of the following factors affect the strength of force experience by a current carrying conduct or

a uniform magnetic field?
(a) Magnetic field strength
(b) Magnitude of current in a conductor
(c) Length of the conductor within magnetic field
(d) All of above

(vi)Find the value of the current in the circuit shown in Fig.

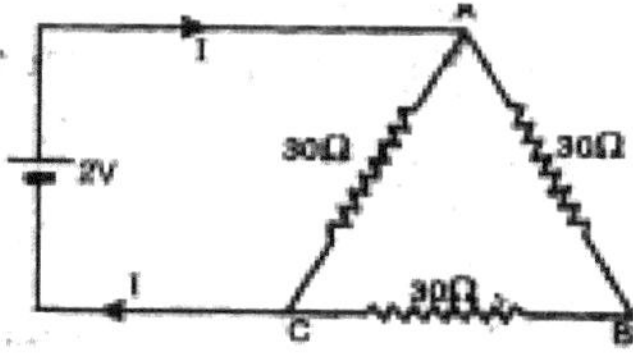

(a)0.3 A
(b)0.1 A
(c)0.5 A
(d)0.2 A

(vii)The change from solid to vapour directly at a constant temperature is called:
(a)Condensation
(b) Regelation
(c) Vaporization
(d) Sublimation

(viii)The greatest power of ionization is in
(a)Alpha particles
(b)Gamma particles
(c)Beta particles
(d)None of above

(ix) Lamps of 40-watt 60 watt are connected in parallel, the total power of combination is
(a)40-watt
(b)60 watt
(c) 24 watt
(d)none

SECTION - II [30 marks]

(Attempt any three questions from this sections)

2. (i) (a)Differentiate between resonance and forced vibrations.
(b) The wavelength of waves produced on the surface of water is 20 cm. If the wave velocityis 24 ms^{-1}, calculate:
(i). The number of waves produced in one second and
(ii). The time required to produce one wave.
(ii). The values of current I flowing in a given resistor for the corresponding values of potential difference Vacross the resistor are given below.

I (amperes)	0.5	1.0	2.0	2.5	3.0	4.0
V(volts)	0.1	0.2	0.4	0.5	0.6	0.8

Plot a graph between V and I and calculate the resistance of that resistor.

(iii). A piece of brass of mass 200 g and at 100° C, is placed in 400 g of turpentine oil, contained in acopper calorimeter of mass 50 g at 15°C. The final temperature recorded is 23°C. Find the specific heat capacity of turpentine oil. Take specific heat capacity for brass = 370 J kg^{-1} K^{-1} and specific heat capacityof copper 390 J kg^{-1} K^{-1}.

3.

(i) What will be the result of mixing 400 g of copper chips at 500° C with 500 g of crushed ice at 0° C?(Sp. heat capacity of copper = 0.42 J g^{-1} $^0C^{-1}$, specific latent heat of fusion of ice = 340 J g^{-1}.

(a) What is meant by radioactivity?

(b) What is meant by nuclear waste?

(c) Suggest one effective way for the safe disposal of nuclear waste.

4 (i) A drill of power $400W$ makes a hole in a lead cube of specific heat capacity $0.13Jg^{-1}C^{-1}$ in $80s$. If the temperature of lead rises from $27°C$ to $327°C$, calculate the mass of lead cube.

(ii). The alongside circuit diagram shows three resistances $2\Omega, 4\Omega$ and $R\Omega$ connected to a battery of emf $2V$ and internal resistance 3. A main current of $0.25A$ flows through the circuit:

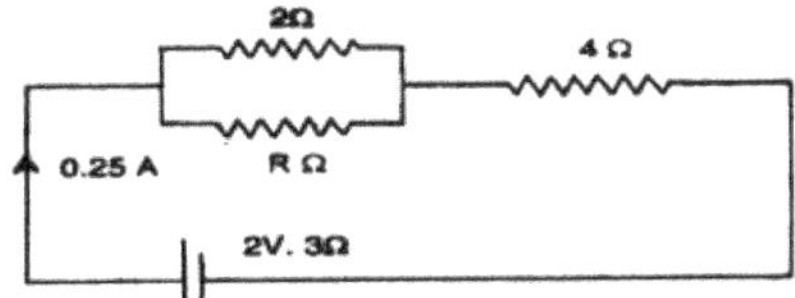

(a) What is the P.d., across the 4Ω RQ resistor?

(b) Calculate the Pd., across the internal resist

(c) What is the P.d., across the R Ω or the 2Ω (d) Calculate the value of R

5 (iii) Complete the following nuclear changes:

(b) $^{24}_{11}Na \rightarrow -Mg + {}^{0}_{-1}\beta$

(c) $^{b}_{a}X^{*} \rightarrow -X + \gamma$

(d) $^{S}_{x}P \rightarrow -Q + {}^{4}_{2}He$

(e) $^{a}_{x}P \rightarrow -Q + {}^{0}_{-1}\beta$

(f) $^{238}_{62}P \longrightarrow -\theta \longrightarrow Q \xrightarrow{-\beta} - R \xrightarrow{-\beta} - S.$

5.(i) With reference to the diagram given below, calculate: The equivalent resistance between P and Q.

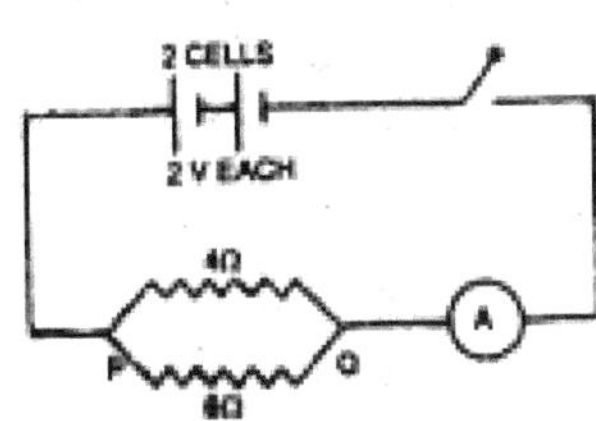

(a) The equivalent resistance between P and Q.

(b) The reading of the ammeter.

(c) The electrical power between P and Q.

(ii) (a) Draw a labelled diagram to show the various components of a step-down transformer.

(b) State the main difference between a step-up and step-down transformer.

(iii). (a) In winter, the weather forecast for a certain day was 'severe frost'. A wise farmer watered his yieldsthe night before to prevent frost damage to his crops. Why did he water his fields?

(iv). (b) X J of heat energy boils off 9 g of water at 100°C to steam at 100°C.
Find the specific latent heat of steam in term of X.

ICSE SEMESTER 2 EXAMINATION
MODEL PAPER 03
PHYSICS
(SCIENCE PAPER 3)

Maximum Marks: 40
Time allowed: One and a half hours

Attempt all questions **from Section A** and any three questions from **Section B**.
The intended marks for questions or parts of questions are given in brackets [ ].

SECTION A[10 marks]
(Attempt all questions.)

Question 1

Choose the correct answers to the questions from the given options. (Do not copy the question, Write the correct answer only.)

(i) Resistance of a metallic conductor does not depend on its
(a)Length
(b)Nature of the material
(c)Area of cross-section
(d)Mass

(ii) Lenz devised a rule to find out the direction of
(a) Current induced in a circuit
(b) Electromagnetic difference
(c) Potential difference
(d) Flow of power in fuse

(ii) The number of protons inside nucleus represents
(a)Atomic mass
(b)Atomic number
(c)Atomic count
(d)Radioactivity

(iii) Two sounds A and B are of frequencies f and 2f respectively. Then:
(a) Both sounds are identical
(b) B is grave, A is shrill
(c) B is shrill, A is grave
(d) B is louder than A

(iv)The presence of the magnetic field at a point can be detected by:
(a)A strong magnet
(b)A solenoid

(c)A compass needle
(d)A current-carrying wire

(v)In India the potential difference between live wire and neutral wire is
(a)240 V
(b)250 V
(c)280 V
(d) 220 V

(vi)The slope of voltage (V) versus current (I) is called

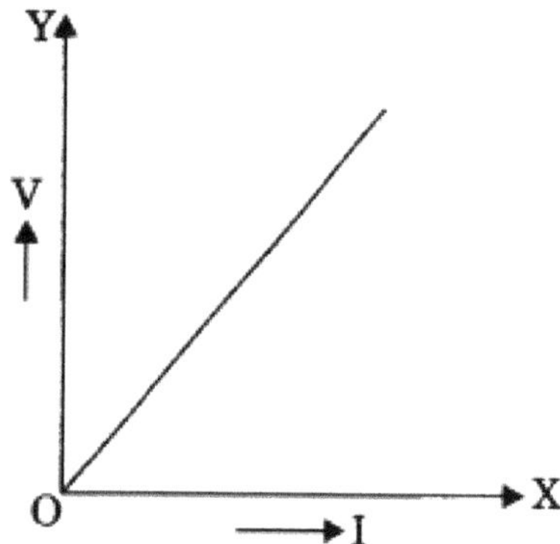

(b) resistance
(c) conductance
(d) resistivity
(e) conductivity

(vii) A piece of ice of mass 40 g is dropped into 200 g of water at 50°C. Calculate the final temperature of water after all the ice has melted. The specific heat capacity of the water = 4200 J/kg°C, specific latent heat of fusion of ice = 336×103 J/kg.
(a)38.33°C
(b)48°C
(c)18°C
(d) 28.33°C

(vii)The insulation colour of earth wire is
(a) blue
(b) red
(c) green
(d) white.

(viii)A soft iron bar is inserted inside a current-carrying solenoid. The magnetic field inside the solenoid:
(a) Will decrease
(b) Will increase
(c) Will become zero
(d) Will remain the same

(ix)Two sounds of same loudness and same pitch produced by two different instruments differ in their:
(a) Amplitudes
(b) frequencies
(c) Wave forms
(d) all the above

SECTION – B [30 marks]

(Attempt any three questions from this sections)

2. (i) (a) Under what condition does the resonance occur?

(b)Why is a loud sound heard at acoustic resonance?

(c) How are colour, wavelength and frequency of light dependent on one another? [3]

(ii) Three resistors are connected to a 6 V battery as shown in the figure. Calculate: **[3]**

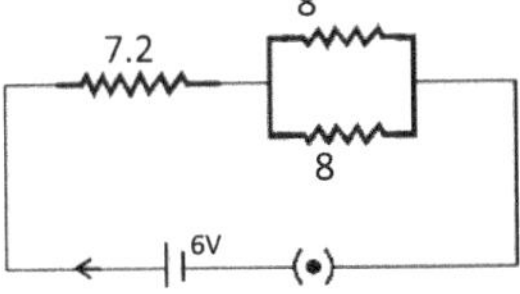

(a) The equivalent resistance of the circuit.
(b) total current in the circuit.
(c) potential difference across the 7.2Ω resistor.

(iii). Water falls from a height of 50 m. Calculate the rise in the temperature of water when it strikes the bottom. (Take $g = 10\ m/s^2$; specific heat capacity of water = 4200 J/kg°C). [4]

3. (i) (a) Name two factors on which the magnitude of an induced e.m.f, in the secondary coil depends.[3]

(b) In the adjacent diagram, arrow shows the motion of coil towards the bar magnet.

1. State in which direction the current lows: A to B or B to A?
2. Name the law used to come to the conclusion.

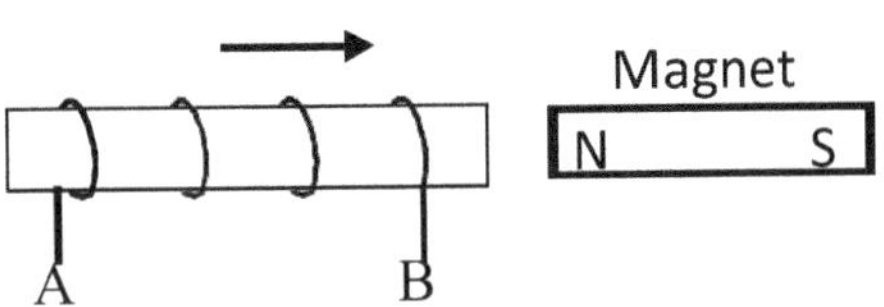

3. Arrange α, β, and γ rays in ascending order with respect to their?

(a) speed (b) mass
(b) Biological effect

(ii) Some ice is heated at a constant rate and its temperature is recorded after every few seconds, till steam is formed at 100°C. Draw a temperature time graph to represent the change. Label the two-phase changes in your graph.

4. (i) (a) Name the transformer used in the power transmitting station of a power plant. [4]

(b)What type of current is transmitted from the power station?

(c)At what voltage is this current available to our household?

(ii) A battery of emf 12 V and internal resistance 2 Ω is connected with two resistors A and B of resistance 4 Ω and 6 Ω respectively joined in series. **[3]**

Find:

(a) Current in the circuit. (b)The terminal voltage of the cell.

(c) The potential difference across 6 Ω Resistor. (d) Electrical energy spent per minute in 4 Ω Resistor.

(iii)10g of water at 20° C to ice A refrigerator converts 100 at –10°C in 35 minutes. Calculate the average rate of heat extraction in terms of watts.

Given: Specific heat capacity of ice = 2.1 J g^{-1} ° C^{-1}. Specific heat capacity of water = 4.2 J g^{-1} ° C^{-1}. Specific latent heat of fusion of ice = 336 J g^{-1}. [3]

5. (i) The relationship between the potential difference and the current in a conductor is stated in the form of a law. [4]

(a) Name the law. (b) What does the slope of I-V graph for a conductor represent?

(c) Name the material used for making the connecting wire.

(ii) Distinguish between the free (or natural) and forced vibrations.

(iii)(a) A metal drill of power output 500W drills a hole in a lead cube of mass 0.25 kg in 6.5 s. The specific heat capacity of lead is 130 J /kg $^{0}C^{-1}$ Calculate:

(b) the heat generated by the metal drill in one second.

(c) the heat generated by the metal drill in 6.5 seconds.

(d) the heat absorbed by the cube in terms of t, if t°C is the rise in temperature of the lead cube.

ICSE SEMESTER 2 EXAMINATION
MODEL PAPER 04
PHYSICS
(SCIENCE PAPER 4)

Maximum Marks: 40

Time allowed: One and a half hours

Attempt all questions from Section A and any three questions from Section B.

SECTION A [10 marks]

(Attempt all questions.)

Question 1

Choose the correct answers to the questions from the given options. (Do not copy the question, Writethe correct answer only.)

(i) What is the condition of an electromagnetic induction?

(a) there must be a relative motion between the coil of wire and galvanometer

(b) there must be a relative motion between the galvanometer and a magnet

(c) there must be a relative motion between galvanometer and generator

(d) there must be a relative motion between the coil of wire and a magnet

(ii) Which of the following is the purpose of connecting a battery in an electric circuit?

(a) To maintain resistance across the conductor

(b) To vary resistance across the conductors.

(c) To maintain constant potential difference across the conductor.

(d) To maintain varying potential difference across the conductor.

(iii) In all the electrical appliances, the switches are put in the

(a) live wire

(b) earth wire

(c) neutral wire

(d) all of above

(iv) An electric iron draws a current 4 A when connected to 220 V mains. Its resistance must be

(a) 1000 Ω

(b) 55 Ω
(c) 44Ω
(d) None of these

(v) A battery of 10 volt carries 20,000 C of charge through a resistance of 20 Ω. The work done in 10 secondsis

(a) 2×10^3 joule
(b) 2×10^5joule
(c) 2×10^4 joule
(d) 2×10^2 joule

(vi)What mass of a solid of specific heat capacity 0.75 J g^{-1}°C^{-1} will have heat capacity 93.75 g/°C.

a) 12.5g
(b) 120g
(c) 105g
(d) 125g

(vii)Two resistors are connected in series gives an equivalent resistance of 10 Ω. When connected in parallel,gives 2.4 Ω. Then the individual resistance are

(a) each of 5 Ω
(b) 6 Ω and 4 Ω
(c) 7 Ω and 4 Ω
(d) 8 Ω and 2 Ω

(viii)The resistivity does not change if
(a) the material is changed
(b) the temperature is changed
(c) the shape of the resistor is changed
(d) both material and temperature are changed

(ix)An electric motor is a device which transforms
(a) Mechanical energy into electrical energy
(b) Electrical energy into mechanical energy
(c) Kinetic energy into potential energy
(d) Electrical energy into Potential energy

(ix)Voice of a friend is recognized by its:
(A) Pitch
(B) quality
(C) Intensity
(D)velocity

SECTION - B [30 marks]

(Attempt any three questions from this section.)

2. (i) What is meant by acoustic resonance? Give one example. [3]

(ii). Five resistors each of 3 Ω, are connected as shown in **figure**. Calculate the resistance:

(a) between the points P and Q.

(b) between the points X and Y. [3]

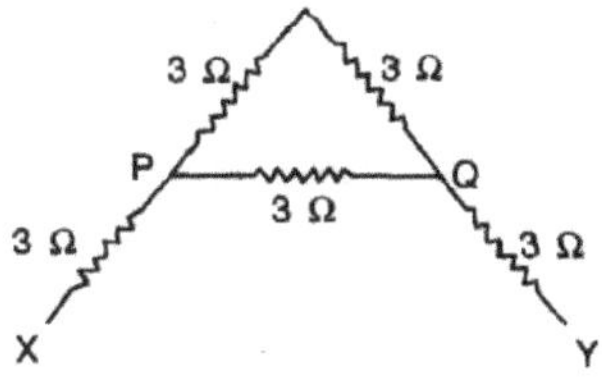

(iii). (a) State two characteristics of a primary coil of a step-up transformer when compared to the secondarycoil (b) With about a D.C. motor, state: 1. The energy change that takes place. 2. The principle on which it operates. [3]

3. (i) (a) Why does a bottle of soft drink cool faster when surrounded by ice cubes than by ice cold water, both at 0°C?

(b) A certain amount of heat Q will warm 1 g of material X by 3°C and 1 g of material Y by 4°C. Which material has a higher specific heat capacity? [3]

(ii). A nucleus $^{A}_{Z}X$ emits an alpha particle followed by g emission; there after it emits two particles to form X_3

(a) Copy and complete the values of A and Z for X_3:

$^{A}_{Z}X \xrightarrow{a} X_1 \xrightarrow{\gamma} X_2 \xrightarrow{2\beta} \cdots X_3$ [3]

... 3

(b) Out of alpha (α), beta (β) and gamma (γ) radiations -

1. which radiation is the most penetrating?
2. which radiations are negatively charged?

(iii) An electrical appliance is rated 1500 W, 250 V. This appliance is connected to 250 V mains. Calculate: [3]

(iv) (i)the current drawn, (ii) the electrical energy consumed in 60 hours, (iii) the cost of electrical energy consumedat `2.50 per kWh. [3]

4. (i) (a) Draw a neat labelled diagram of an a.c. generator.

(b) What is the magnitude of the emf induced in thecoil when its plane becomes parallel to the magnetic held? [4]

(ii) An immersion heater of 396 W, changes 60 g of ice at -12°C into water at 40°C. If the specific heat capacity of ice is 2 J $g^{-1}\,{}^0C^{-1}$, calculate the specific latent heat of fusion of ice, when the heater is switched on for 1 min and 20 s. [3]

(iii)A vibrating tuning fork is placed over the mouth of a burette filled with water. The tap is opened and thewater level gradually falls. It is observed that the sound becomes the loudest for a particular length of air column.

(a) What is the name of the phenomenon taking place when this happens?

(b) Why does the sound become the loudest?

(c) What is the name of the phenomenon taking place when sound is produced for another length of air column and is not the loudest? [3]

5. (i)For the combination of resistors in figure find the equivalent resistance between (a) C and D, (b)A and B [4]

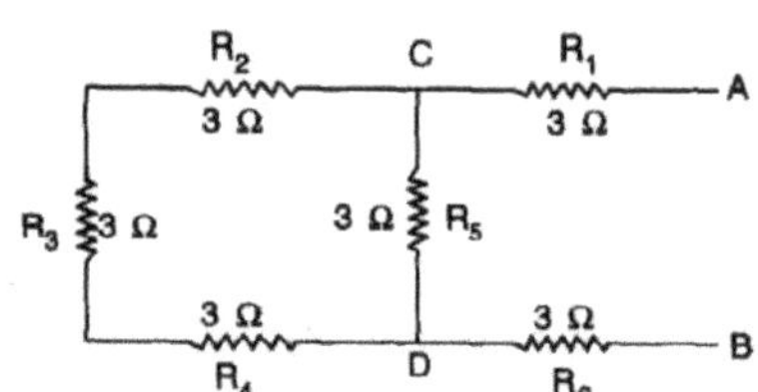

(ii) Two bulbs A and B are rated 100 W, 120 V and 10 W, 120 V respectively. They are connected across a 120 V source in series. Calculate the current through each bulb. Which bulb will consume more energy? [3]

(iii) A lead bullet travelling with a speed of 80 m/s strikes an unyielding target and is brought to rest. The kinetic energy of the bullet is converted in to heat which is absorbed by the bullet itself Calculate the rise oftemperature of bullet. Specific heat capacity of lead = 130 J $kg^{-1}C^{-1}$.[3]

ICSE SEMESTER 2 EXAMINATION
MODEL PAPER PHYSICS
(SCIENCE PAPER 5)

Maximum Marks: 40

Time allowed: One and a half hours

Attempt all questions from Section A and any three questions from Section B.

SECTION A [10 marks]

(Attempt all questions.)

Question 1

Choose the correct answers to the questions from the given options. (Do not copy the question, Writethe correct answer only.)

(i) The greatest power of ionization is in

(a)alpha particles

(b)gamma particles

(c)beta particles

(d)none of above

(ii) A wire of resistance 4R is bent in the form of a circle. What is the effective resistance between the ends of diameter?

(a) 2R

(b) 3R

(c) 1R

(d) 1.5R

(iii) In the process of melting,

(a)heat energy is given out

(b)heat energy is absorbed

(c) there is no change in heat energy

(d) heat energy is first given and then absorbed

(iv) The most important safety method used for protecting home appliances from short circuiting or overloadingis by

(a) earthing

(b) use of fuse

(c) use of stabilizers

(d) use of electric meter.

(v) A cooler of 1500 W, 200 volt and a fan of 500 W, 200 volts are to be used from a household supply. The rating of fuse to be used is

(a) 2.5 A

(b) 5.0 A
(c) 7.5 A
(d) 10 A

(vi) Among the following properties of a wave, the one that is independent of the other is its___.
(a)amplitude
(b)velocity
(c)frequency
(d)wavelength

(vii)$_7N^{14}$ and $_7N^{15}$ represents.
(a)isotopes
(b)isotones
(c)isobars
(d)isosters

(viii)In an experiment to verify ohm's law current in the circuit is varied by: (i) changing the battery (ii) varying the resistance in rheostat
(a) Only (i) is true
(b) Only (ii) is true
(c) Both (i) and (ii) are true
(d) None of (i) and (ii) are true

(ix)When salt is added to water, then its boiling point.
(a)decreases
(b)increases
(c)remains the same
(d)depends on the amount of the salt added

(x)An isotope is used in the treatment of cancer.
(a)uranium
(b)cobalt
(c)iron
(d)iodine

SECTION – B [30 marks]

(Attempt any three questions from this section)

2 (i) In a laboratory experiment to measure specific heat capacity of copper, 0.02 kg of water at 70 °C was poured into a copper calorimeter with a stirrer of mass 0.16 kg initially at 15 °C. After stirring, the final temperature reached to 45°C. Specific heat of water is taken as 4200 $Jkg^{-1}\,°C^{-1}$. [3]
(a) What is the quantity of heat released per kg of water per 1 °C fall in temperature.
(b) Calculate the heat energy released by water in the experiment in cooling from 70 °C to 45 °C.
(c) Assuming that the heat released by water is entirely used to raise the temperature of calorimeter from 15 °C to 45 °C, calculate the specific heat capacity of copper.

(ii). $^{27}_{12}Mg \rightarrow Al \xrightarrow{\gamma}$ [3]

In the above ı ıclear reaction. (i) $_{90}Th^{234}$ emits α, β -particle and is transformed to X. What is the mass number and the atomic amount of X. (ii) X emits γ ray. What is the resulting nucleus?

(iii) One kilogram of ice at -10^0 C is heated until the whole of it vaporises. How much heat is required? Specific
latent heat of fusion of ice = 336×10^3 J kg^{-1}, specific latent heat of steam = 2268 x 10^3 J kg^{-1}, specific heat capacity of ice = 2.1 ×10^{3}J/kg ^{0}C, specific heat capacity of water = 4.2 × 10^{3}J/kg ^{0}C. [4]

3.(i) The V-I figure for a series combination and for a parallel combination of two resistors is as shown in the figure above. Which of the two, A or B, represents the parallel combination? Give a reason for your answer.

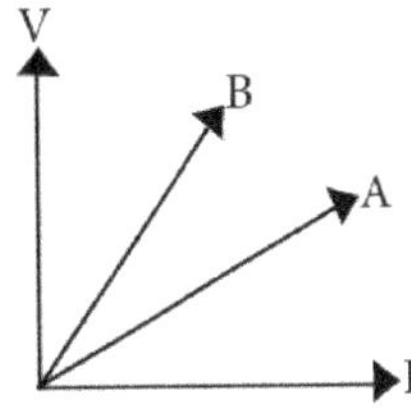

[3]

(ii) A stringed musical instrument, such as The Sitar, is provided with a number of wires of different thicknesses. [3]

Explain the reason for this.

(iii). The following diagram shows a coil X connected to a sensitive centre-zero galvanometer G and a coil P connected to a d.c. supply through a switch S. Describe the observation when the switch S is

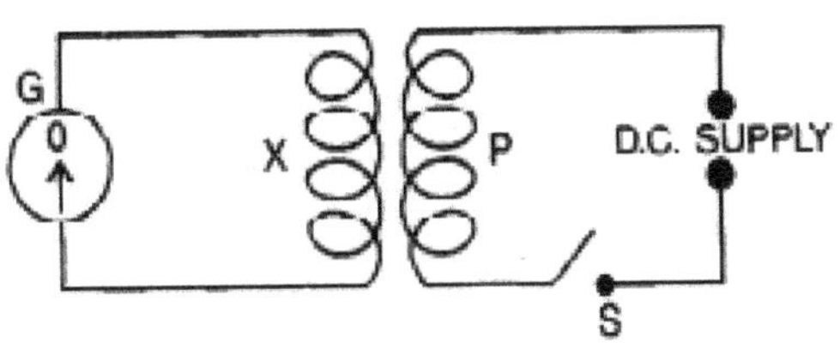

(a) closed suddenly, (b) then kept closed,
(c) finally opened. Name and state the law which explains the above observations. [4]

4. (i) In the nuclear reaction given below, nucleus x changes to another nucleus y.

$^{226}_{88}x \rightarrow y + \alpha +$ energy

(a) What is the atomic and mass numbers of Y?
(b) Name the gas formed when the α -particle acquires two electrons.
(c) What is the effect on the motion of the α -particle when it passes through a region containing a magnetic field? [4]

(ii). (a)A tuning fork held over an air column of a given length, produces a distinct audible sound. What do you call this phenomenon? How does it occur?
(b) Explain why musical instruments like the guitar are provided with a hollow box. [3]

(iii) 40 g ice at -10°C is heated by a heater of power 250W, such that water formed from it, attains the temperature of boiling point. For how long the heater is switched on? Take the specific heat capacity of ice = 2 J g^{-1} $^{0}C^{-1}$and the specific latent heat of ice 340 J/ g. [3]

5. (i) (a) Name the material used for making a fuse wire. State two properties of the material of fuse-wire which make it suitable for use. (b) Calculate the electrical energy in SI units consumed by a 100 W bulb and a 60 W fan connected in parallel for 5 minutes. [4]

(ii) Some hot water was added to three times its mass of cold water at 10°C and the resulting temperature was found to be 20°C. What was the temperature of the hot water? [3]

(iii) Three resistors 6.0 Ω, 2.0 Ω, and 4.0 Ω respectively joined together as shown in the fig. The resistors are connected an ammeter and to a cell of e.m.f. 6.0 V. Calculate:(i) the effective resistance the circuit. (ii) the current drawn from the cell. [3]

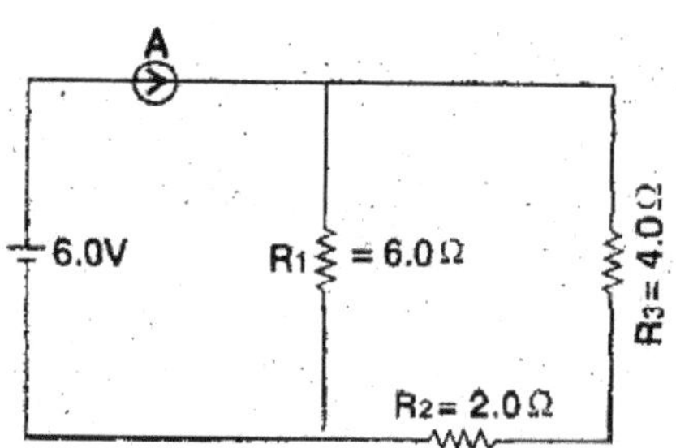

ICSE SEMESTER 2 EXAMINATION
MODEL PAPER PHYSICS 06
(SCIENCE PAPER 6)

Maximum Marks: 40
Time allowed: One and a half hours

Attempt all questions from Section A and any three questions from Section B.

SECTION A [10 marks]
(Attempt all questions.)

Question 1

Choose the correct answers to the questions from the given options. (Do not copy the question, Writethe correct answer only.)

(i)The heat generated by current carrying conductor does not depend upon the.

(a)length of the wire
(b)strength of the current
(c)area of cross section of the wire
(d)mass of the wire

(ii)The value of boiling point of water in kelvin scale is.

(a)273 K
(b)373K
(c)473K
(d)173 K

(iii)A conductor of resistance 3 Ohm is stretched uniformly till its length is doubled. If the wire is bent in the formof an equilateral triangle, find the resistance across any side.

(a) 8/1 Ohm
(b) 8/4 Ohm
(c) 3/8 Ohm
(d) 5/8 Ohm

(iv) By reducing the amplitude of a sound wave, its:

(a) Pitch increases
(b) loudness decreases
(c) loudness increases
(d) pitch decreases

(v) the amount of heat released when 5.0 g of water at 200C is changed into ice at 00C. (Specific heat capacity of water = 4.2 J/g°C, Specific latent heat of fusion of ice = 336 J/g).

(a) 2100J
(b) 2500J
(c) 2400J
(d) 2000J

(vi) material is used to prepare the filament of a bulb.

a) Tungsten
b) Lead
c) Copper
d) Platinum

(vii) A soft iron bar is inserted inside a current-carrying solenoid. The magnetic field inside the solenoid:

(a) Will decrease
(b) Will increase
(c) Will become zero
(d) Will remain the same

(viii) An electric bell is a device which transforms

(a) Mechanical energy into electrical energy
(b) Electrical energy into sound energy
(c) Kinetic energy into potential energy
(d) Electrical energy into Potential energy

(ix) A body of mass 1 kg falls from a height of 100 metre. If its all mechanical energy is changed into heat, then heat produced will be.

(a) 350 cal
(b) 150 cal
(c) 60 cal
(d) None

(x) The specific latent heat of melting of ice is:

(a) 80 cal g^{-1}
(b) 2260 J g^{-1}
(c) 80 J g^{-1}
(d) 336 J kg^{-1}

SECTION - B [30 marks]

(Attempt any three questions from this Section.)

2. (i)A liquid of mass 100 g and at 120°C is poured in water at 20°C, when the final temperature recorded is40°C. If the specific heat capacity of the liquid is 0.8 J g^{-1} $^{0}C^{-1}$, calculate initial mass of water. [3]

(ii). (a) State any two measures to minimize the impact of global warming.

(c) What is greenhouse effect? [3]

(iii) A cell of 1.5 V and internal resistance 1.0 Ω is connected to two resistors of 4.0 Ω and 20.0 Ω in series as shown in the fig. Calculate the-

(a) current in the circuit. [4]

(b) potential difference across the 4.0-ohm resistor.

(c) Voltage drops when the current is flowing.

(d) potential difference across the cell.

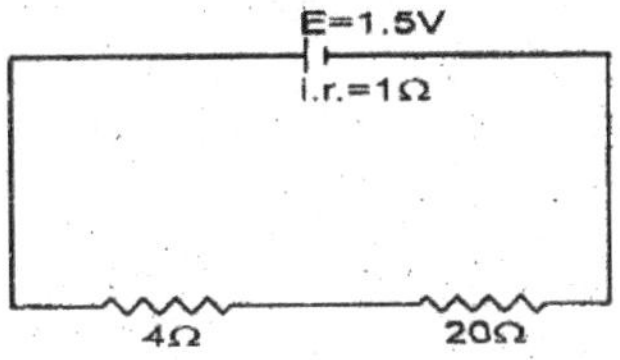

3. (i) Copy and complete the following nuclear equations by filling in the correct values in the blanks.

$$^{233}_{92}P \xrightarrow{\alpha} - Q \xrightarrow{\beta} - R \xrightarrow{\beta} - S$$ [3]

(ii) (a) Name the transformer used in the power transmitting station of a power plant.

(b) What type of current is transmitted from the power station? [3]

(c) At what voltage is this current available to our household?

(iii) A heating coil is immersed in a calorimeter of heat capacity 50 J $^{0}C^{-1}$ containing 1.0 kg of a liquid of specific heat capacity 450 J kg^{-1} $^{0}C^{-1}$. The temperature of liquid rises by 10 ^{0}C when 2.0 A current is passed for the 10 minutes. Find: (a) the resistance of the coil, (b) the potential difference across the coil. State the assumption used in your calculations. [4]

4. (i) The diagrams (a) and (b) given below are of a plug and a socket with arrows marked as 1, 2, 3 and 4, 5,6respectively on them. Identify and write Live (L), Neutral (N) and Earth (E) against the correct number. [4]

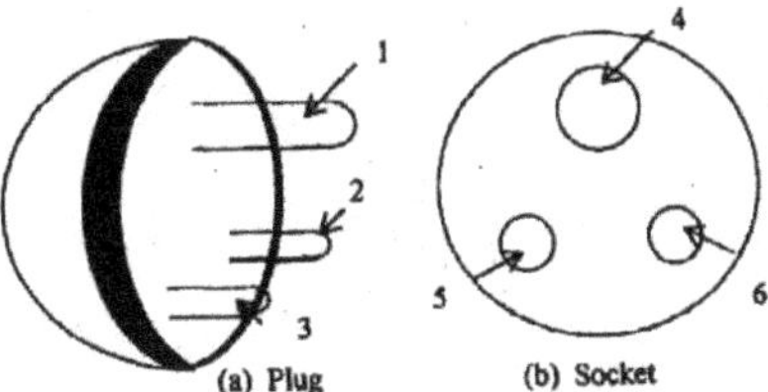

(ii) The temperature of 600 g of cold water rises by 15 ^{0}C when 300 g of hot water at 50 ^{0}C is added to it. What was the initial temperature of cold water? [3]

(iii) The adjacent figure shows a circuit. When the circuit is switched on, the ammeter reads 0.5 A.

(a) Calculate the value of the unknown resistor R.

(b) Calculate the charge passing through the 3 Ω resistor in 120s. (c) Calculate the power dissipated in the 3 Ω resistor.

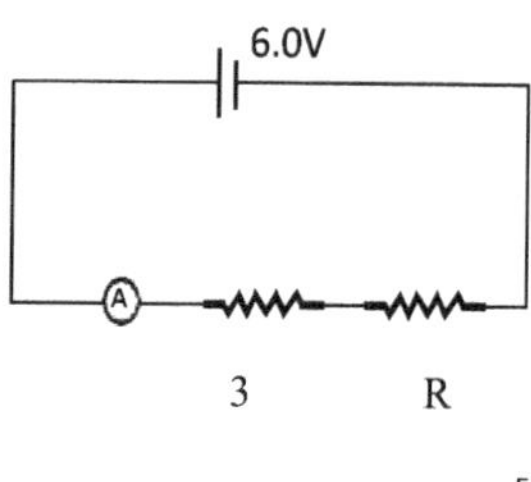

[3]

ICSE SEMESTER 2 EXAMINATION
MODEL PAPER-07
PHYSICS
(SCIENCE PAPER 1)

Maximum Marks: 40

Attempt all questions from Section A and any three questions from Section B.
The intended marks for questions or parts of questions are given in brackets [ ].

SECTION A [10 marks]
(Attempt all questions.)

Question 1

Choose the correct answers to the questions from the given options. (Do not copy the question, Write the correct answer only.)

(i) Name the radiation which has the lowest speed.
(a) Alpha radiations
(b) beta particle
(c) gamma particle
(d) none of these

(ii) galvanometer is connected with circuit in connection.
(a) Series
(b) Parallel
(c) Either series or parallel
(d) None of these

(iii) Which of the following has maximum current?
(a) 100W-220V
(b) 10W-220V
(c) 200W-200V
(d) 300W-250V

(iv) 5 g of ice at 0°C is dropped in a beaker containing 100 g of water at 60°C. The final temperature will be
(a) 32°C
(b) 16°C
(c) 8°C
(d) none

(v) A quantity of heat required to change the unit mass of a solid substance, from solid state to liquid state, while the temperature remains constant, is known as
(a) Latent heat
(b) Sublimation
(c) Hoar frost
(d) Latent heat of fusion

(vi) The release of energy from the sun is due to
(a)nuclear fission
(b)nuclear fusion
(c)burning of gases
(b)chemical reaction

(vii) Find the value of the current between AB in the circuit shown in Fig.

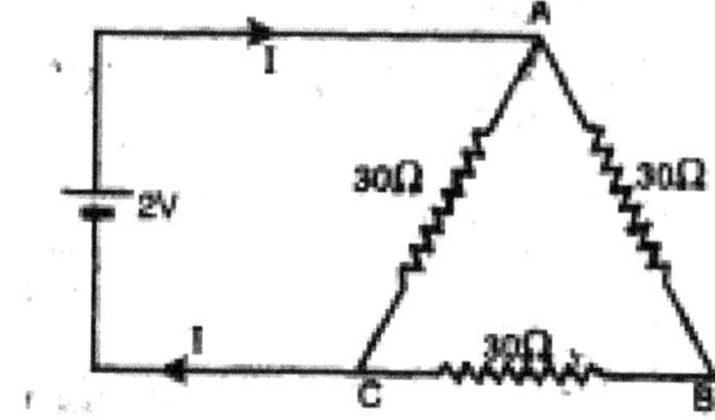

(a) 0.3 A
(b) 0.1 A
(c)0.5 A
(d) none

(vii) On reversing the direction of current in a wire, the magnetic field produced by it:
(a)Gets reversed in direction
(b)Increases in strength
(c)Decreases in strength
(d)Remains unchanged in strength and direction

(viii)A battery of 12V is connected in series with resistors of 0.2-ohm, 0.3 ohm,0.4 ohm,0.5 ohm and 12 ohms. How much current would flow through the 0.3-ohm resistor
(a)0.895A
(b)1.11A
(c)0.5A
(d)0.8 A

(ix) Electric power does not depend on
(a)resistance
(b)voltage
(c)current
(d) temperature

(ix) Transformers only work with
(a)direct current (DC)
(b)alternating current (AC)
(c)charges
(d)radioactive substances

(x) Which of the following is not an example for free vibrations?
(a)If the bob of a simple pendulum is disturbed, it oscillates about its mean position.

(b)A load suspended from a spring when compressed and released, oscillates about its mean position.
(c)A stretched string when plucked at its midpoint executes oscillations.
(d)Vibrations of the diaphragm in a radio speaker

SECTION B [30 marks]

(Attempt any three questions from this Section.)

Question 2

In fig. A and B represent the particle displacement with distance when waves pass through air. What is the realtion between their (i) velocities, (ii) wavelength, (iii) pitch and (iv) loudness? [3]

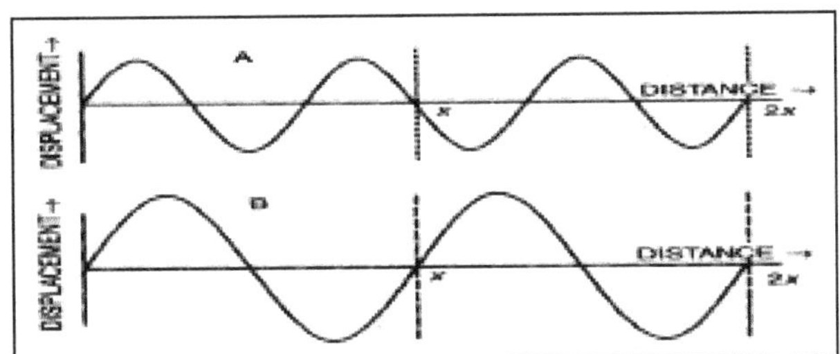

(ii) Derive an expression for the electric power connecting: [3]

(a) current and resistance.
(b) current and potential difference.
(c) resistance and potential difference.

(iii) Explain principle of calorimetry **[4]**

Question 3

(i) How many alpha and beta particles are emitted when Uranium nucleus decays to Lead [3]

(ii) An electric bulb is rated at 250 V. 100W. What is its resistance? What maximum current can be passed through it? [3]

(iii) A particular resistance wire has a resistance of 3.0 ohm per metre. Find: **[4]**

(a) The total resistance of three lengths of this wire each 1.5 m long, in parallel.
(b) The potential difference of the battery which gives a current of 2.0 A is each of the 1.5 m lengths when connected in parallel to the battery (assume that the resistance of the battery is neglible).

(c) The resistance of 5 m of a wire of the same material but with twice of the area of cross section.

Question 4

(i) Calculate the mass of steam at 100°C that must be passed into 8.4 kg. of water at 30°C to raise the temperature of water to 80°C. [Sp. heat capacity of water Q = 4.2 J/g°C, Sp. latent heat of vaporisation of steam = 2268 J/g.] [4]

(ii)(a) What is the name given to a cylindrical coil whose diameter is less in comparison to its length?

(b) If a piece of soft iron is placed inside the current carrying coil, what is the name given to the device?

(c) Give one use of the device named by you in (b) above. [3]

(iii)Calculate the amount of ice which is required to cool 150 g of water contained in a vessel of mass 100 g at 30 °C, such that the final temperature of the mixture is 5 °C. (Take specific heat capacity of material of vessel as 0.4 J/g°C, specific latent heat of fusion of ice = 336 J/ g, specific heat capacity of water =4. 2

J/g°C). [3]

Question 5

(i) A substance is in the form of a solid at 0°C. The amount of heat added to this substance and the temperature of the substance are plotted on the following graph:

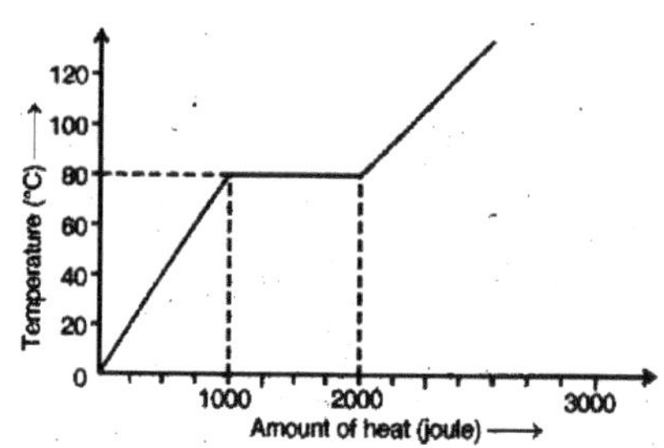

If the specific heat capacity of the solid substance is 500 J/kg °C, find from the graph:
(a) the mass of the substance;
(b) the specific latent heat of fusion of the substance in the liquid state. [4]

(ii)In the nuclear reaction given below, nucleus x changes to another nucleus Y.

A. What is the atomic and mass numbers of Y?

B. Name the gas formed when the α-particle acquires two electrons.

C. What is the effect on the motion of the α-particle when it passes through a region containing a magnetic field? [3]

(iii) Three resistors of 6.0, 2.0 and 4 respectively are joined together as shown in the figure. The resistors are connected to an ammeter and to a cell of e.m.f. 6.0 V. Calculate:

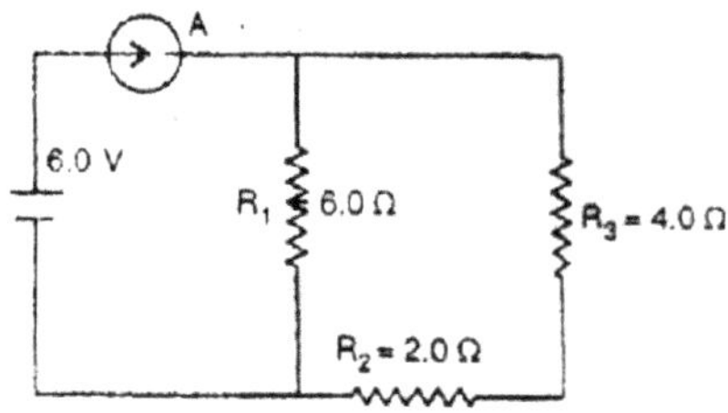

(a) the effective resistance of the circuit.
(b) the current drawn from the cell. [3]

www.ingramcontent.com/pod-product-compliance
Ingram Content Group UK Ltd.
Pitfield, Milton Keynes, MK11 3LW, UK
UKHW061959290726
14090UKWH00021B/1288